$10.00

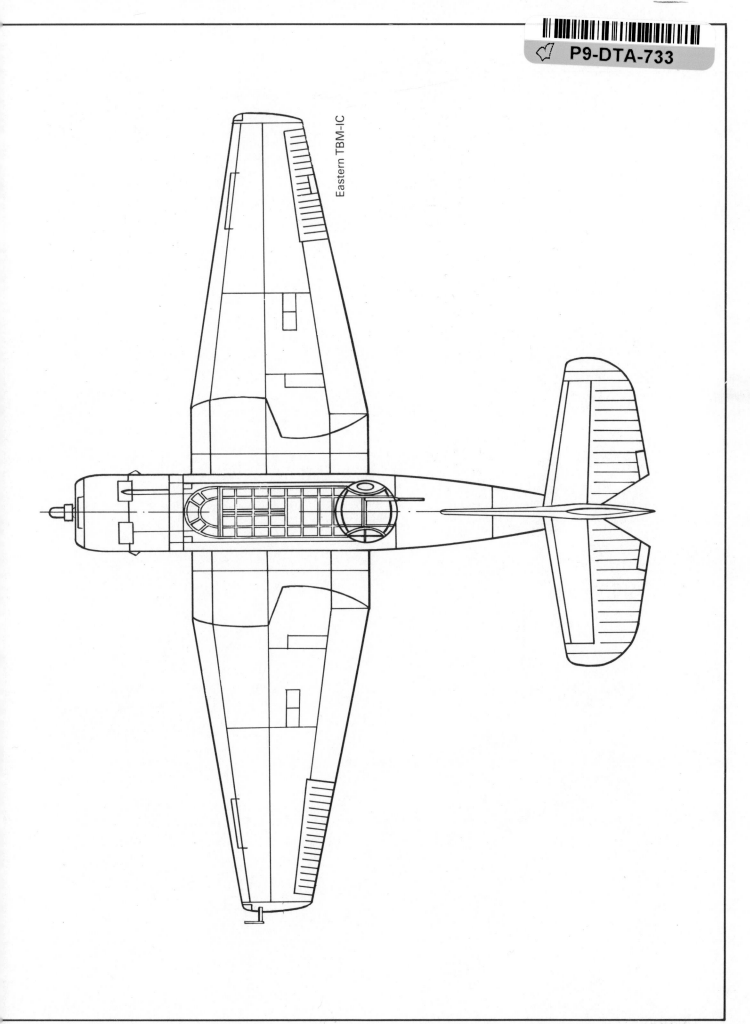

Eastern TBM-IC

AVENGER
AT WAR

AVENGER
AT WAR

Barrett Tillman

Charles Scribner's Sons
NEW YORK

First U.S. edition published by
Charles Scribner's Sons, 1980

1 3 5 7 9 11 13 15 17 19 I/C 20 18 16 14 12 10 8 6 4 2

Printed in Great Britain
Library of Congress Catalog Card Number 79-89682
ISBN: 0-684-16452-3

**Dedicated to my friends William
N. Hess and Richard M. Hill**

Below: TBFs and F6Fs of Air
Group 5 aboard USS *Yorktown*
(CV-10) during a training cruise
in 1943. / *Grumman*

Bibliography
Gallery, Daniel; 'No Rest for the Subs', *Wings of Gold*; August 1976
Lord, Walter; *Incredible Victory*; Harper and Row, New York, 1967
Polmar, Norman; *Aircraft Carriers*; Doubleday, New York, 1969
Stafford, Edward; *The Big E*; Dell Paperbacks, New York, 1964
Thruelsen, Richard; *The Grumman Story*; Praeger, New York, 1976

Contents

Foreword

Vice-Admiral William I. Martin
USN (Retired)

Ernie Pyle was perhaps the best-known war correspondent of World War II. Because he had a knack for being in the thick of the hottest action, his observations were always poignant and colourful. What Ernie said about aircraft carriers seemed to apply to the Avenger:

'It lacks almost everything that seems to denote nobility, yet deep nobility is there. It has the lines of a cow — it doesn't cut through, knifing along — it just ploughs. Yet a carrier is a ferocious thing, and out of its heritage of action has grown its nobility.'

Originally the Avenger was designated a torpedo bomber. However, many TBF squadrons shifted the emphasis to other means of attack, and with good reason. If the US had possessed reliable aerial torpedoes, the TBF would have been known as a great torpedo plane because it was stable, easy to fly, and 'honest'. But because aerial torpedoes were notoriously unreliable — of 31 dropped by my squadron, none ran hot, straight, and normal — many torpedo squadrons adopted dive bombing tactics. Thank heaven the Grumman Iron Works built them strong!

The Avenger was our first carrier attack plane to be equipped with radar. It had an immediate impact on tactics. Initially it was used for special purposes on a small scale such as night combat air patrol teams and as pathfinders leading attack missions through bad weather. Finally, after an *Enterprise* TBF squadron executed a highly successful night masthead bombing attack on Japanese shipping in Truk lagoon, the Navy designated *Enterprise* a night carrier with an air group composed of radar-equipped Avengers and Hellcats.

The Avenger's career covered barely 12 years, but it did nearly everything in the book and did them well — in the Atlantic,

Pacific, Mediterranean, Arctic and Indian Oceans.

Those who have read Barrett Tillman look forward to this book. They appreciate his uncommon ability to characterise an airplane in a fast-paced operational history without belabouring technical details. Readers are surprised to learn that the author is still in his 20s. It is astonishing that such experience in vintage aircraft — not to mention an exciting writing skill — should be found in one so young.

Introduction

They called it the Turkey. Not a flattering name, even when mixed with affection, considering that the turkey is one of nature's less accomplished fliers. But the TBF-TBM seldom enjoyed much fame, and certainly not much glory. Though it fought a global war, the Avenger spent much of its career just as most men spent that conflict: engaged in routine, unspectacular duties, waiting for something to happen.

As with any aircraft history, the tale is more of the men than the airplane. And that is as it should be. For like the Avenger, too many of these men have been overlooked for too long. And never have I encountered a more deserving group of individuals. Their wartime contributions, no matter how diverse or how far removed from combat, are overdue for recognition. Therefore, it is gratifying for me to help bring to light the accomplishments of some of those who designed, built, maintained, and flew the TBF and TBM. Their talent, dedication, and energy remain an inspiration.

Some deserve extra acknowledgement for their invaluable assistance. And the adjective 'invaluable' is not chosen lightly. My special friend, Vice-Admiral Bill Martin, was so encouraging and so helpful from the very beginning that the project went far beyond the original concept. In that respect, much of the credit for this book belongs to him. He knew the Avenger well, for as a bold and skilful aviator he employed it effectively by day and by night. There is no one I would rather have written the Foreword, and I am grateful for his eloquent contribution.

Admiral Martin also put me in touch with other Avenger people, both from the Navy and from Grumman. Chief among them is Ralph Clark, whom I tend to regard as Mister TBF. In his capacity as Grumman's field service representative, he probably knew the Avenger as well as anyone ever did. Ralph's knowledge is fully matched by his enthusiasm, for he took time off from his duties in Grumman's Washington, DC office to escort me to Bethpage, Long Island — the TBF's birthplace. There I was treated to the splendid assistance of H. J. 'Schony' Schonenberg, the company historian.

Grumman's history department sets an example for the aerospace industry to follow. One simply cannot say enough nice things about the wonderful folks at Bethpage.

Documentary assistance came largely from my valued friends at the Navy's Operational Archives in Washington, DC. Squadron reports were made available, as were two studies made during the 1940s. The first was *Naval Air Operations in the Marianas* by H. G. Land and A. O. Van Wyen. The second was Lee M. Pearson's series on the development of naval strike aircraft between the wars. Other published sources are listed in the short bibliography.

Sincere thanks and appreciation are extended to all the others who kindly provided recollections, information and illustrations: Peter M. Bowers; Capt William B. Chace; James H. Farmer; Capt Larry C. French; Charles E. Henderson III; Robert L. Hall; Richard M. Hill; Capt Edward J. Huxtable; Norm Johnson; Robert R. Jones; Arthur Koch; Rear-Admiral M. F. Leslie; Lester T. Ludwig; Michael J. O'Malley; Warren R. Omark; Rear-Admiral Hank Suerstedt; Capt Benjamin C. Tate; Cdr A. H. Vito; Charles B. Westbrook; and John F. Curtis.

Below: **TBF-1, 1942.** / *Grumman*

Behind the Scenes

Men's imagination habitually outstrip their ability to implement their concepts. This situation has existed in all forms of human endeavour, but perhaps seldom as often as in the pursuit of war. For in the race to bring new weapons into existence, technology is forever running behind imagination. Nowhere is this better illustrated than in naval aviation.

In 1911, at the tender age of barely seven years, the powered flying machine was first put to naval use. Early that year, pioneer aviators Eugene Ely and Glenn Curtiss conducted their successful experiments by flying from shipboard and from the water itself. Though years would pass before any aircraft was capable of lifting a worthwhile offensive payload, imaginative officers quickly grasped the potential of the new machine.

One such man was Admiral Bradley A. Fiske of the US Navy. Undeterred by the technical problems standing in his way, by 1912 he had taken out a basic patent for a means of carrying and launching aerial torpedoes. It was a classic example of an idea waiting for technology to catch up.

It remained for the British Royal Navy to match imagination with know-how. The first air-dropped torpedo was launched from a seaplane piloted by Lt Arthur Longmore barely two weeks before the outbreak of World War I. Little more than 12 months later came the first combat test of the torpedo plane.

The 2,650 ton packet *Ben-My-Chree* was converted to a seaplane carrier in 1914 with room for two Short 184 floatplanes. Operating in the Aegean Sea in August 1915, *Ben-My-Chree* made naval aviation history. On 11 August, Flight Commander C. H. Edmonds made a low-level attack on a Turkish merchantman and got a hit with his 14-inch torpedo. A British submarine claimed to have torpedoed the vessel about the same time, so the success could not be credited solely to Edmonds.

A few days later another opportunity arose, and this time there was no doubt. Both Short 184s, led by Edmonds, found targets. Edmonds torpedoed an enemy supply ship and Flt Lt G. B. Dacre hit a tug. Both vessels sank; the initial successes for a new and promising weapon.

During World War I, Britain and Imperial Russia were the world leaders in shipboard aviation, but technical and political changes eventually altered the picture dramatically. By the war's end the seaplane carrier, which Britain and Russia had used effectively, was in decline. The true aircraft carrier emerged in the form of HMS *Furious, Argus* and *Eagle*, leaving Britain clearly in the lead with both ships and aircraft. But within a few years the United States began to catch up.

America commissioned her first aircraft carrier, USS *Langley*, in 1922. The 'Covered Wagon' was a converted collier, with a narrow deck best suited to operating light, single-engine aircraft. This did not prevent aerial torpedo development from pressing ahead, though sometimes it crawled more than it pressed. But that same year there came a dramatic demonstration of the torpedo plane's capability.

On 27 September the Atlantic Fleet's Torpedo and Bombing Plane Squadron conducted a combat exercise 70 miles off Norfolk, Virginia. Land-based PT-1s and PT-2s attacked three battleships with practice torpedoes. Built by the Naval Aircraft Factory in Philadelphia, the PT series was a lumbering, Liberty-engined biplane, slow and ungainly. But though the dreadnoughts manoeuvred at full speed, *Arkansas* and *North Dakota* were both hit — the former no less than seven times. It was conclusive proof that air-launched torpedoes could be dropped safely and function normally.

With commissioning of the 36,000 ton carriers *Lexington* and *Saratoga* in 1927, the US Navy finally acquired a realistic carrier-based torpedo capability. The first of 124 Martin T3M-1s were delivered to Torpedo Squadron 1 in September 1926. Experience aboard the '*Lex*' and '*Sara*' showed a need for certain modifications which were incorporated into the similar T4M-1. Torpedo Squadron 2B took delivery of the initial batch of these 103 aircraft in August 1928. The Martins were all similar in

appearance: big, angular, radial-engined biplanes which would remain little modified throughout their design or development phase. Their main drawbacks were a relatively low speed (114mph) and sluggish climb rate — nearly 15min to 5,000ft for the T4M. But carrier pilots appreciated the type's handling characteristics and good visibility.

In order to spread its limited business as widely as possible, the Navy decided to extend Great Lakes Aircraft a contract for a somewhat improved version of the T4M. In 1929, Great Lakes received an order for 18 TG-1s. But the improvements added weight, particularly the new wing folding mechanism, and top speed fell to under 110mph. A year later still another sub-contractor, Detroit Aircraft Corporation, was allowed to build a streamlined T4M type with a 630hp Wright engine in place of the earlier Pratt & Whitney. It was called the TG-2, and proved capable of more than 125mph. The last of these was delivered to

Above: **The Douglas DT-2 was produced in small numbers from 1921 to 1924. Built by three other firms in addition to Douglas, it was powered variously by the Liberty 400 or 450hp water-cooled engines and by the Wright 650hp in the DT-4 version.** / *Bowers*

Top: The Glenn Martin Company produced 124 T3M-1s and -2s in the late 1920s. They remained in service until 1932, continuing the liquid-cooled engine, biplane design far beyond its prime. / *Bowers*

Above: The T4M-1 was an improved version of the T3M, most easily distinguished by a Wright 575hp or Pratt & Whitney 525hp air-cooled radial engine. Fifty were built by Great Lakes aircraft and designated TG-1 and TG-2. They were still operational as late as early 1938. / *Bowers*

Torpedo Squadron 6 in early 1938, when production for all T4M variants ended with a total of 277 aircraft.

In 1934 the Navy Bureau of Aeronautics released a set of criteria for a new torpedo plane. By then it was realised that the maximum speed to be expected from a traditional biplane design was barely 140kts, or 170mph. Additionally, the trend was towards duplication of roles. The scout-bomber concept, epitomised in the Douglas SBD, was given a counterpart by 1940 in the new torpedo bomber. Both Great Lakes and Douglas entered designs, but since only the latter offered a monoplane, it was the clear leader. The Douglas entry's designation was TBD.

Intended for both torpedo attack and horizontal bombing, the TBD was probably as close to a quantum leap in naval air technology as existed up to that time. With all-metal construction, power folding wings and semi-retractable landing gear, it was more than years removed from the T4M series; it was worlds apart, especially where speed was concerned. The XTBD-1 was clocked at 206mph, or 178kts. From 1937 to 1939, 130 TBD-1s would be delivered to the fleet. Initial recipient was VT-3 assigned to *Saratoga*.

In fairness to the TBD, its wartime misfortune cannot be blamed upon the design. Considered by itself, the Devastator (as it came to be optimistically called) was a good airplane. It was popular with its crews and was easy to fly. The problem was that the Douglas, once the front runner, had been passed by the competition in the endless race for superiority. In 1942 it was still a good aircraft — by 1937 standards.

The TBD's main shortcomings — range and speed — were recognised by the Navy well before Pearl Harbor. And examination of combat experience from the Spanish Civil War convinced the Bureau of Aeronautics that modern attack aircraft required heavier defensive armament as well.

So in 1939 BuAer produced an entirely new design specification for a carrier-based torpedo bomber which could double as a scout. These criteria included a 300mph speed, internal capacity for three 500lb bombs or a torpedo, or enough bomb bay fuel for a 3,000-mile scouting range. Armour plate and self-sealing fuel tanks were also specified. Defensive armament was to include two forward-firing machine guns, a power-driven turret gun and a hand-held ventral gun.

Again there were two entrants, both experienced in building naval aircraft. One was Vought, which had produced a line of biplane and monoplane scout-bombers and was then developing the promising F4U fighter. Its entry was the XTBU-1, later named Sea Wolf.

The other entrant was Grumman.

The Bethpage, Long Island firm had never attempted a torpedo plane before. But the XTBF-1 showed exceptional promise. Chief among these was armamant and ordnance. The Grumman design could accommodate four 500lb bombs instead of the three requested and had a workable electric-powered turret. No other manufacturer had been able to perfect such a feature, as previous attempts employed mechanical or

Above: A new generation arrived in naval aviation with the advent of the Douglas TBD-1, entering squadron service in 1937. All-metal construction, power-folding wings, and semi-retractable landing gear were innovative for US Navy aircraft. / *Bowers*

Left: A TBD-1 of Torpedo Squadron Six off USS *Enterprise* drops a Mk 13 aerial torpedo from low level. Lack of proper testing and technical deficiencies severely limited tactical employment of American torpedoes during early World War II combat. / *Bowers*

11

hydraulic methods. Curtiss-Wright's prototype SB2C dive bomber was originally to have had a powered turret, but neither Curtiss nor its competitor Brewster Aircraft could find a solution for their designs.

Grumman provided armour plate for the power turret's motor and ammunition, and self-sealing fuel lines as well as tanks were installed. To save weight, flight controls were removed from the second pilot's cockpit and flotation bags were replaced by life rafts. Forward armament was reduced to a single .30cal machine gun. The Navy ordered two XTBF-1s on 8 April 1940.

The prototype TBF and TBU were in some respects well matched. But the Grumman was lighter, faster, had more range and was smaller with wings folded. Its full span of 54ft 2in could be reduced to 18ft 4in. Based upon these findings, the Navy opted for the TBF-1, and an order for 286 examples was made in December 1940.

But there were problems to be dealt with. The projected speed for the new bomber was 320mph in prototype form. As development proceeded into the fall of 1941, inevitable weight increases amounting to .5 ton reduced this to some 275mph. And an engineering change was required to compensate for tail-heaviness induced by the extra weight. Finally Grumman extended the engine mount forward an extra 12in to restore longitudinal stability.

Grumman's engineering test pilot Robert L. Hall made the first flight in the XTBF-1, BuAer No 2539, on 7 August 1941. Bob Hall's recollections of the occasion are typically brief:

'This first flight lasted but five minutes and was really only a high-speed taxi test with a short lift-off. The second flight the next day was 10 minutes, and the third the following day lasted 41 minutes.

'During the rest of August and through September and October I flew this same airplane 20 times for a total of 23 hours. I did not fly a TBF again until February 1942 when I did the dive demonstrations at Anacostia and Dahlgren, Maryland.'

Though photographic proof is lacking, veteran Grummanites recall that the first one or two flights were made without a dorsal fin. The factory then fitted a fin to improve stability. But this footnote to Grumman history was overshadowed by the events of 28 November 1941.

On that day, pilot Hobart Cook was flying the prototype with engineer Gordon Israel in the back seat. Apparently a leak developed in the 1,500psi hydraulic system, filling the interior of the plane with a fine mist which was taken for smoke. Cook reported an in-flight fire, and he and Israel bailed out 15 miles from the factory field. Cook made a safe descent but Israel swung into a telephone pole and suffered a broken ankle. The XTBF-1 crashed in scrub oak near Brentwood, New York.

Unlike the aerospace industry today, in the 1930s and 1940s most aircraft companies built only one prototype. Therefore, if the first example was lost, that programme experienced a major setback. The experimental Vought F4U and Curtiss SB2C were both prime examples. But as the Navy had authorised two XTBF-1s, there was hope for keeping on schedule since the second fuselage was nearly complete. Working literally around the clock,

Left: The first production TBF-1, BuNo 00373, in flight on 23 March 1942. / *National Archives*

Below: The instrument panel of the TBF-1 was representative of its day: manifold pressure, ammeter, tachometer, altimeter, airspeed indicator (in knots), gyro compass, turn-and-bank indicator, vertical speed, radio compass, and combination temperature-pressure gauge. Other fixtures are fuel gauges and electrical circuits. / *Grumman*

Bottom: Left side of the TBF-1 cockpit, showing trim controls, arresting hook switch, tail wheel lock, and throttle quadrant. / *Grumman*

Grumman had the second prototype finished within three weeks, and it was test flown on 15 December.

By then, the need was more urgent than ever.

Production of TBF-1s began slowly. The first was delivered in January 1942, and five more followed in February. Torpedo Squadron 8, destined for the carrier *Hornet*, was recipient of the new planes while in training at Norfolk, Virginia. But another delay was encountered in March when the first five or six aircraft were returned to the factory for new wing-folding hinge pins.

Operational testing disclosed some disappointments. With a top speed of about 275mph (228kts) and a service ceiling of some 22,000ft, the TBF-1 fell short of contract requirements. About this time the Bureau of Aeronautics VTB desk recommended production of the TBU, but it came to nothing. The Vought may or may not have proven equal to the Grumman in production form; it was a moot point. For even with its shortcomings, the Grumman had the ultimate, inescapable advantage. It was being delivered when no other torpedo plane was available. Vought was too involved with the Corsair fighter to devote much time to another project.

One aspect of TBF activity during early 1942 was almost overlooked. Partially as a means of simplifying identification, partially as a morale booster, the Navy assigned popular names to most of its aircraft. This was the period when the TBD was optimistically called the Devastator. TBF project engineer Arthur Koch wanted to call 'his baby' the Revenger, knowing it would have the opportunity to pay back the Pearl

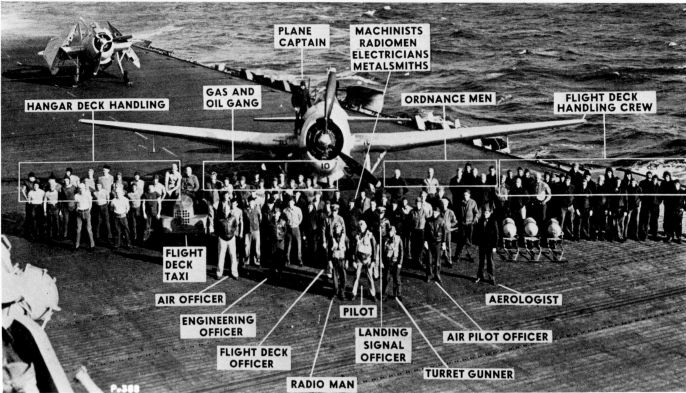

PLANE CAPTAIN

MACHINISTS RADIOMEN ELECTRICIANS METALSMITHS

HANGAR DECK HANDLING

GAS AND OIL GANG

ORDNANCE MEN

FLIGHT DECK HANDLING CREW

FLIGHT DECK TAXI

AIR OFFICER

ENGINEERING OFFICER

FLIGHT DECK OFFICER

PILOT

LANDING SIGNAL OFFICER

RADIO MAN

TURRET GUNNER

AEROLOGIST

AIR PILOT OFFICER

Top: **An early production TBF-1 over Long Island Sound in early 1942. The second pilot's controls were deleted after the 50th production machine.** / *Grumman*

Above: **A dramatic illustration of the air and ground team necessary to put a plane aloft on a combat mission. There are over 90 men behind the three-man flight crew.** / *Grumman*

Harbor attack. The Navy did not adopt Koch's idea, but it came close. The TBF became the Avenger.

Production is the basic aspect of aviation history which is often ignored, but it is a big part of the Avenger story. By June 1942, Grumman was building 60 TBFs per month, and first exceeded 100 in November. The first year's production totalled 646, and during 1943 Grumman maintained an average of nearly 150 per month. But the F6F Hellcat had priority among the Grumman designs, and in early 1942 arrangements were made for Eastern Aircraft Division of General Motors Corporation to take over slowly Avenger production.

Trepidation existed in the aviation industry about giving such work to automobile manufacturers. The close tolerances and precision mating of aircraft

parts seemed to some observers beyond the capability of most auto builders, at least on a massive scale. Previous experience tended to reinforce this attitude, as thousands of aircraft engines — most notably Wrights — were built by automobile plants under subcontract. Poor quality control early in the war led to an unenviable reputation for Wright engines. Aviators said they were 'externally lubricated' due to excessive oil leakage. The fact was, Wrights were no more inherently unreliable than any other engines. The difference was in how they were manufactured and assembled.

But Eastern Aircraft proved a pleasant surprise. Its vast experience in mass production techniques, combined with Grumman's methods of simplifying assembly processes, made a winning team. The first TBM-1s were actually GM-assembled aircraft composed of Grumman-supplied parts. One was completed in November and two in December 1942. Thirty-one were built in the first three months of 1943, after which General Motors production grew in astonishing leaps. TBM deliveries accelerated rapidly during mid-year, with 75 units in June and 100 in July. Thus, GM had achieved the 100 per month figure in 10 months; slightly faster than the parent firm.

Both Grumman and Eastern accomplished their production records with large numbers of inexperienced workers. Nearly all of the wartime factory employees were completely new to aviation. Therefore, Grumman and GM had to rely upon their small cadres of

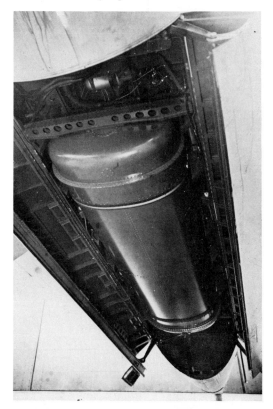

experienced professionals to make the job of building airplanes as simple as possible. Both companies maintained close co-operation throughout the war, insuring that problems were solved as efficiently as possible.

In fact, there were relatively few difficulties. During the second half of 1943 GM's Trenton, New Jersey plant was turning out Avengers in amazing quantities. So many, in fact, that TBM production outnumbered TBF deliveries for the first time in September: 160 to 156. The TBF's peak month came in October with 163, when GM had a temporary setback and cropped to 107 TBMs. But in November, Eastern doubled its previous month's output with 215 Avengers, and Grumman delivered 135. This total of 350 remained the peak month of the entire programme for nearly a year. Then in December Grumman built the last 39 TBFs, for a two-year total of 2,291.

Throughout 1944, Eastern produced an average of nearly 10 TBMs every day. By January 1945 the monthly delivery rate was up to 350, and peaked at exactly 400 in March. But the rapid Japanese capitulation in mid-August brought an almost immediate halt to Avenger production, when 328 were delivered. In September only 24 TBMs were completed, and they were the last of the line.

In all, nearly 10,000 Avengers were built from 1942 to 1945. The breakdown was as follows:

	TBFs	TBMs	Total
1942	646	3	649
1943	1,645	1,109	2,754
1944	—	3,481	3,481
1945	—	2,953	2,953
Total	2,291	7,546	9,837

The Avenger was produced in larger numbers than any other naval strike aircraft of World War II — or, for that matter, of all

Left: An innovative feature of the prototype TBF was this jettisonable bomb bay fuel tank. It enabled the Avenger to serve as a long-range reconnaissance aircraft, and provided an ideal ferrying capability. / *Grumman*

Below: Apparently still uncompleted, this very early TBF-1 is waiting its port wing-tip antenna and application of the rudder stripes. Note that the port underwing national insignia has not been painted yet.
/ *Grumman*

time. It remains outnumbered only by the Corsair and Hellcat among all US Navy aircraft, as both fighters exceeded 12,000 examples. And it is noteworthy that another Grumman-Eastern product owns fourth place, as nearly 8,000 Wildcats were delivered from 1940 to 1945. These were followed by some 7,500 Helldivers and nearly 6,000 Dauntlesses. Therefore, of roughly 55,000 World War II era carrier-type aircraft built in the US, Grumman designs amounted to more than half.

The only comparable record is the near monopoly which Douglas designs had on carrier attack aircraft during the late 1950s and early 1960s, with the A-1, A-3 and A-4.

Left: This oft-printed 1942 publicity shot has become one of the best-known TBF photos, as five Avengers fly through spectacular cumulus cloud formations. / *Grumman*

Right: The XTBF-3 did not enter production as such, but served as prototype for the TBM-3, built by Eastern Aircraft Division of General Motors Corporation. Three-quarters of all Avenger production was accomplished by Eastern, as Grumman ceased building TBFs in December 1943 to concentrate on Hellcats. / *Grumman*

Below: An excellent close-up of a TBF-1, showing to advantage the gun port for the single .30cal firing through the prop arc. Demands for more firepower led to installation of .50cal in the wings. / *Grumman*

To War

The Battle of Midway has most frequently been told from the viewpoint of the ill-fated Torpedo Squadron 8. Lt-Cdr John Waldron led 15 TBDs from the carrier *Hornet*, and all were destroyed attacking the Japanese carriers. Only one man, Ensign George Gay, survived. The fact that an entire squadron was wiped out made a deep impression on the American public, and it has been a prominent feature of every generalised account of the battle.

Both of the other TBD squadrons involved, VT-3 from *Yorktown* and VT-6 from *Enterprise*, suffered nearly as heavily. In fact, none of Torpedo 3's aircraft returned to base. Ten were shot down and the two survivors ran out of fuel before reaching the US task force. Of *Enterprise's* 14 torpedo planes, three returned to the ship, but one was so badly damaged that it was pushed overboard. Thus, of 41 TBDs which launched on the strike of 4 June, only two returned safely.

Midway was the end for the TBD. The losses there amounted to 30% of the total production and, coupled with previous attrition, there were too few remaining for continued use.

Fortunately, the TBF was on hand. But the Avenger's combat debut was little improvement over the misfortune of the Devastator. And there lies the other half of the tragedy that was Torpedo 8.

When *Hornet* departed the east coast of the US, part of her torpedo squadron remained behind. This detachment was responsible for putting the first production TBF-1s into operational status at Norfolk, Virginia. The usual 'bugs' had to be worked out of the new aircraft, and by the first week in May VT-8 (Detached) was still at Norfolk. Then on 8 May all 19 Avengers were ordered to the west coast for shipment to Hawaii.

The intention was to put the TBFs aboard *Hornet* in time for the upcoming battle. US intelligence knew the Japanese would

Below: **With a 30-knot relative wind, a TBF could get off a carrier deck with little trouble.**

attempt to occupy Midway Atoll and the war's most important fleet engagement quickly shaped up. But the Avengers literally 'missed the boat' by one day. They arrived in Hawaii on 29 May, the day after *Hornet* sailed for Midway.

The detachment went ashore to Luke Field on Ford Island, part of the massive Pearl Harbor navy base. But there was little time to settle in, for a day later volunteers were needed to fly six TBFs out to Midway.

Lt Langdon K. Fieberling was the officer in charge of the Midway contingent of VT-8. At 0730 on 1 June he took off, leading five other Avengers flown by Ensigns C. E. Brannon, A. K. Earnest, O. J. Gaynier, V. A. Lewis and an enlisted pilot, NAP D. D. Woodside. Each TBF had a radioman and a gunner, and two planes carried navigators. Some of the young ensigns had never flown beyond sight of land before.

The 1,300 statute miles from Oahu to Midway were covered in eight hours, an average groundspeed of 160mph or almost 140kts. The six Avengers landed at 1530 Pearl Harbor time and were almost immediately armed with torpedoes. With

little else to do, the crews decided to improve the armament of their planes by adding 'wing guns'. Actually, these were merely strips of tape applied to the leading edges of the wings to simulate gun muzzles.

For the next two days Fieberling's crews manned their planes at dawn to be in readiness should the Japanese appear. On the morning of the third day, the enemy showed up.

Ensign Albert K. Earnest was the only VT-8 (Detached) pilot who survived the battle. His brief report, made on 23 June 1942, describes the action:

'On the morning of 4 June, we manned our planes as usual at 0400, warmed them up, cut the engines and prepared to stand by during the morning alert. At 0545 I was told by a Marine officer to start my engine, as unknown planes had been sighted by a patrol plane 100 miles from Midway.

'At 0600 we taxied out, took off and joined up in two three-plane sections, planes and sections stepped down. We set out on a course of 320° True, at an airspeed of 160kts indicated, at an altitude of 2,000ft. Approximately five minutes after take-off we

Above: **Pilots of VT-8 inspecting one of the first TBF-1s delivered to the Navy in January and February 1942. Many of these early Avengers were returned to the factory for work on their wing-folding mechanisms.**
/ Grumman

were attacked by two or three enemy planes, one of which I tentatively identified as a Messerschmitt Bf109 fighter. We evaded these planes, climbed to 4,000ft, and continued on our course.

[Intelligence reports erroneously stated the Japanese Navy was using Bf109s aboard its carriers. Similar sightings were reported during the early months of the war, but they were of course incorrect.]

'At approximately 0700 we sighted the enemy force about 15 miles away, headed for Midway Island. It was a force of about 10 ships; destroyers, cruisers, and at least one battleship forming a screen around two long carriers. Just as we sighted the enemy fleet we were attacked by a large force of enemy fighters. We immediately started a dive at full throttle through clouds to within 150ft of the water and headed directly for the carriers. The enemy fighters, which seemed to outnumber us at least three to one, were Zero fighters and Messerschmitts. They continued to attack us and on the second burst hit my turret gunner, AMM3c J. D. Manning, putting him out of action and eventually killing him. At the same time my hydraulic system was shot away, causing my tail wheel to drop down and blank out my tunnel gun.

Right: Avenger at war. Navy crewmen on Midway Atoll tend to the only TBF to return of six which attacked the Japanese carriers on 4 June 1942. The pilot, Ensign A. K. Earnest, brought back this badly-damaged aircraft with his gunner dead and radioman wounded. / *Grumman*

Below: Another view of Earnest's aircraft, which force-landed on the beach. Note battle damage to the starboard wing-tip and bent prop tips. / *National Archives*

'Soon after this my tunnel gunner, RM3c H. H. Ferrier, was hit on the head and although dazed and bleeding, was not seriously injured. I received a small cut on the right cheek, apparently by shrapnel from an explosive shell.

'When we were still several miles from the Japanese carriers, my elevator wires were shot away. I released my torpedo at the nearest ship, a light cruiser, as I thought I was out of control, but regained control with the elevator tab before hitting the water. I could not see whether or not my torpedo hit the cruiser.

'Two enemy fighters chased me for about 10 minutes after this, and although they made runs on me as well, no vital parts of the plane were hit and it continued to perform very well. After the enemy planes left me, I looked back at the enemy fleet and could see no signs of any ships having been hit. I then returned to Midway and was forced to make a crash landing, since both of my wheels would not come down. None of the other TBF-1 airplanes returned to the base.'

The six Avengers had attacked at approximately the same time as 27 Marine dive bombers and four Army B-26 Marauders. None of these planes inflicted any damage upon the Japanese armada, which was considerably larger than Earnest's vantage point showed. In all, there were four carriers, two battleships, three cruisers, and 12 destroyers. Without a co-ordinated plan or fighter support, the 37 American planes had little chance of success. Including five of the six Avengers, 19 planes of this attack were shot down.

But they served a purpose. The enemy's operations schedule was disrupted by this attack, and was further delayed by the three TBD squadrons which arrived about two hours later. As a result, the Japanese air groups were still aboard their carriers, fully armed and fuelled, when three squadrons of Dauntless dive bombers struck. The *Enterprise* and *Yorktown* SBDs knocked out three of the four Japanese carriers in about five minutes, and the fourth was sunk late that afternoon.

Though the TBF's combat debut was hardly the 'devastating success' which later publicity claimed, the new torpedo plane had begun to live up to its name: Avenger.

21

Tech Rep

W. Ralph Clark

During World War II most aircraft companies maintained field service representatives to liaise between the manufacturer and the military. These 'tech reps' were civilians who served in the military branch to which they were attached. They helped their 'customers' with new products and developed operational or maintenance procedures while performing trouble-shooting chores as well. Most tech reps shuttled between operational units and the factories, keeping the flow of information moving. But a few spent more time in forward areas than many soldiers or sailors. One such was Ralph Clark, who put in four years in the Pacific, both in Hawaii and aboard aircraft carriers. He was Grumman's representative for the Avenger and later for the Hellcat. He came to know both aircraft intimately, as he recalls here:

'I applied to Gruman in June of 1941 and was taken on in July. I had graduated from college in May. After I was accepted on 10 July I went through the regular two-week check-out course to see if you knew how to work with metal. How to hit a piece of aluminium with a hammer, a lot of things like that. Since I had been in metalsmithing before, I had an advantage over a lot of other applicants.

'At the time of the Battle of Midway, near the first weekend in June 1942, Grumman's general manager Jake Swirbul made a speech. That Friday he got everybody together on the apron in back of the plant and stood up on a work bench with a

Below: **Mock-up of the XTBF-1 in original form, without the dorsal fillet. The first prototype is thought to have flown once or twice without the fillet, which became standard on all subsequent TBFs.** / *Grumman*

Above: Yankee ingenuity. Indistinct but visible is the .50cal machine gun mounted on the wingroot of Lt-Cdr W. I. Martin's TBF-1. Grumman tech rep Ralph Clark helped a VT-10 ordnanceman make this rough modification in response to a demand for more firepower during 1943. / *Grumman*

microphone. He said, "There's a big battle going on out there, and the Navy's in trouble. We have to give them every airplane we can by Monday. So I want everybody in the place to work until you can't work anymore." We turned on and took every spare part we could find, everything we could put together, and on Monday morning there were 22 new airplanes sitting out on the line. All different types, but mostly F4Fs and TBFs.

'I had become involved with the TBF almost immediately after joining the company. They were putting a group together in the experimental shop under Steve Baloch, one of Grumman's mechanical geniuses. Steve wanted somebody who was above average in knowledge because this difficult airplane was about to be undertaken. In college I had studied physics and did very well on my mechanical aptitude test, so they assigned me to Steve to work with him on the TBF.

'Actually, we were mainly concerned with building the power turret. Oscar Olsen was the engineer. The problem was how to provide power for the turret, and Oscar had the right idea. He called his old friends at General Electric, who made amplidynes for moving large structures like drawbridges and cranes. Oscar asked if GE could make small amplidynes we could use to move the turret, and they said they could. So Oscar was the engineer, Steve Baloch was the mechanical expert who put it all together and I was his assistant. We also had two Italian boys, Sam and Frank Ficarro. They were very good metalsmiths, like old world artisans who could do anything with a file or chisel. Their work looked like it came out of a jewelry shop.

'Jake Swirbul had a saying. He said, "If an airplane doesn't fly, fix it. If you can't fix it, tell us." That was Jake. And when TBFs arrived in the fleet in spring 1942, the Navy had never seen a power turret before, and they had trouble with it. So they asked Grumman to send somebody out to Pearl

Harbor to help maintain and service the turrets. That's how I got in the picture. Since I was 22 and still single, and knew the turret very well, I became the TBF service representative, assigned to ComAirPac at Pearl Harbor.

'The first thing I realised at Pearl Harbor was that I couldn't instruct every sailor, so I talked to ComAirPac staff and suggested we set up a turret school. We took one spare turret out of supply and set it up in a frame in a hut at Kaneohe Naval Air Station. A mechanical electrician from Pearl Harbor was sent over to help me install the wiring, and we set up our school. As the TBF squadrons came in, they sent us their ordnance men and turret operators, and it worked fine.

'We had all kinds of limit switches and safety stops in that turret. We had to, if we didn't want these kids shooting off the tails of their airplanes. Oscar had worked on the problem and these features were involved, but well designed. For instance, when the gunner let up on the trigger, we didn't want the barrel sticking out to one side unnecessarily so there was a return-to-neutral switch. Another item was the little star wheels that were actuated by small pins as they moved around the mounting ring. Now and then one of the star wheels would get out of line and cause some trouble, but otherwise it worked great. We never had any more turret headaches.

'After the school was going, I became involved with the whole airplane almost immediately. The oil system, the hydraulics, you name it. But there was one episode I'll never forget. The TBF-1s had only one .30cal machine gun firing forward, through the prop arc, and the pilots wanted more firepower than that. You couldn't blame them, especially when they were attacking destroyers or cruisers with lots of AA guns and the Japanese were throwing everything but their anchors at our boys. It wasn't very good for morale of either the pilots or the rest of the squadron.

'So I got to know Bill Martin, who was then CO of Torpedo Squadron 10. Bill was a very brave man. He always led his squadron in an attack and did an awful lot of flying himself. He never assigned his executive officer or flight officer to lead a mission if he could help it. As a result, Bill told me he wanted some .50cals firing forward to keep the Jap gunners' heads down.

'There was a young ordnanceman first class named Martin — no relation to Bill — who figured a way to mount a .50 cal on each wing of a TBF. He designed some brackets of angle iron and wanted to attach them to the skin of the airplane. That's where I got in the act. I said that we'd better be careful, because we didn't want to rip the wings off when the guns fired, and we didn't want to rupture the fuel bladders which were beneath the spot at the wingroot where these guns would go. The fuel cells held 79gal right beneath the aluminium skin of the wing. So we bolted the U-shaped angle iron right to the skin, just as tight as we could make it. The tails of the bolts under the skin were what I had to protect the fuel tanks from so they wouldn't puncture the self-sealing tanks. We put rubber tape on the bolts to protect the tanks, and it seemed to work.

'Then it was a matter of installing an interrupter gear on the two guns so they wouldn't shoot holes in the prop. The whole setup was strictly Rube Goldberg, with the ammo belts out in the open. We only modified Bill's airplane this way, but eventually later models of TBFs and the TBMs had a .50cal in each wing as normal equipment.

'The single biggest problem we had, both to the fleet and to us at Grumman, was the hydraulics. Previously our airplanes mainly had vacuum flaps, mechanical flaps or, as in the F4F, mechanical cranking of the landing gear. Also manual folding of the wings, so everything before the TBF had been vacuum or manual. We now moved into completely hydraulic operation, which was a whole new field.

'I had an instant Avenger repair kit in the trunk of my car in Hawaii. Using small envelopes of hydraulic seals, I was able to nearly double the number of airworthy airplanes by just supplying the right seal at the right time. What happened was that the bomb bay door cylinders or landing gear actuator cylinders would get pinched and would start to leak. For some reason, the Navy had not got a large enough supply of the right seals out to the fleet. A mechanic would put in a request for the particular seal and would get back a slip marked NIS — Not In Stock. They hadn't got that far in the supply system yet.

'So Grumman would mail me envelopes of

Left: **Two divisions of TBFs on a training flight in Florida during 1942.** / *Grumman*

hydraulic seals after I told them what was needed. And with a big brown envelope filled with various small seals, we were able to put up additional airplanes almost every day. It was a major breakthrough just to have enough hydraulic seals available.

'We occasionally had a structural problem, but not very many. I don't recall much trouble with the wing folding mechanism. The legend is that Mr Grumman designed that system using a rubber eraser and a paperclip he'd bent out of shape. This was for the Wildcat, but the same principle applied to our other airplanes.

'I do remember one problem when we were shifting Avenger production to General Motors for the TBM. The Navy had developed glide bombing, in which they approached a target at 50° instead of the 70° angle they used for the SBDs. Theoretically, this 50° glide was to be used by TBFs when torpedoes weren't reliable enough and they had to use bombs. The SBDs carried one 1,000lb bomb but the TBF carried two 1,000lb or four 500lb, which was a pretty good load for those days.

'I rode with Bill Martin and some of his boys in VT-10, and they were half crazy. The airplane was supposed to be redlined at 315kts in a dive (370mph) but they were getting up to 370kts (425mph). It worked most of the time in TBFs, but some of the early TBMs had trouble. A couple of airplanes ripped their wings off. I was temporarily back in the States at that time, working at NAS Jacksonville, Florida, which had TBFs. Fort Lauderdale, a nearby base, had TBMs. Their skipper was Joe Taylor, who had led Torpedo 5 from the old *Yorktown* in the Battle of the Coral Sea. Joe got hold of me and said two of his TBMs had pulled their wings off while glide bombing and the crews were killed. They went right into the ocean.

'Finally we found a TBM which had a partially bent wing. It was just what we were looking for, since the wing hadn't failed, but it showed us where the wing was overstressed. We took that wing off the airplane, put it on a railroad car, and sent it to Grumman. The factory took the wing apart and analysed it. They found that the rivet pattern had been changed at General Motors for production purposes. As a result, they had lost some of the original strength. Naturally, the necessary changes were made on Eastern's production line. But other than that, they did a great job. They even had their own service department with their own reps. So I think they did a good job. As good as you could do with that R-2600 Wright engine.

'You had to be careful how you operated the cowl flaps on the 2600. If you let it cool too fast, it could hang up. Some of the valves would flake or chip and you'd have to change a cylinder. We didn't have as much trouble with it as the PBM flying boats did, with their tight cowls. But once you got the TBF airborne and closed the cowl flaps, you generally didn't have anything to worry about.'

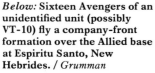

Below: **Sixteen Avengers of an unidentified unit (possibly VT-10) fly a company-front formation over the Allied base at Espiritu Santo, New Hebrides.** / *Grumman*

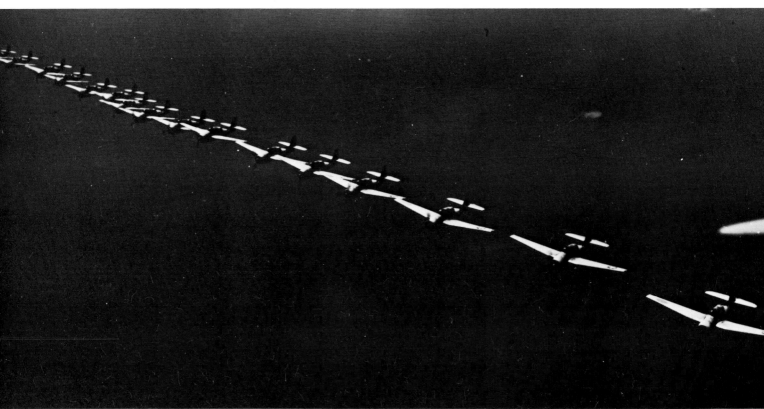

First Successes

The Avenger was blooded at Midway — all too literally — but got two more chances at Japanese carriers during 1942. Both opportunities were associated with the long, bitter, Guadalcanal campaign.

US Marines opened the first American offensive of the war on 7 August 1942 when they landed on Guadalcanal in the southern Solomons. Three carriers lent air support to this operation: *Saratoga, Enterprise* and *Wasp*. The TBF units were Torpedo Squadrons 3, 7 and 8. Their duties consisted mainly of scouting and ground support, as there was little else for them to do.

Ironically, one of the best-known incidents of the TBF's career is widely thought to have occurred on 7 August. In fact, it did not happen at all — not where any Avengers were concerned.

Japanese reaction to the unexpected American assault was swift. Mitsubishi Betty bombers and Zero fighters from Rabaul flew southward to attack the US ships off Guadalcanal. Combats were fought over a wide area of sky, with casualties inflicted on both sides. One of the Japanese pilots was a flight petty officer named Saburo Sakai. He claimed a Dauntless and a Wildcat shot down in the early part of the mission, then he spotted a formation of eight US planes, which he identified as F4F Wildcats.

Sakai approached the 'Wildcats' from below and behind, steadily closing the range. In his book *Samurai*, published in 1957, Sakai describes his shock when he realised his intended victims were not F4Fs, but TBFs. He even described the gunners' turrets and deep bellies. Then the American gunners opened fire at about 50yds and caught his Zero in a deadly cross-fire. Badly wounded, his plane heavily damaged, Sakai pressed through the formation and then somehow managed to return over 600 miles to Rabaul. His injuries kept him out of combat for nearly two years.

Sakai attributed his identification error to the family resemblance between the Wildcat and the Avenger. But it was a more serious error than that. The bombers were not TBFs, but SBDs of Bombing Squadron 6 off *Enterprise*. Sakai's wingmen said he shot down two of the bombers during his brief combat, but *Samurai* correctly states that no Avengers were lost this day. The reason is that Sakai committed two recognition errors!

Actually, the lone SBD he shot down was the only Dauntless lost on 7 August. And while it would be small consolation, Sakai did hit two of the VB-6 aircraft during his short, close-range gunfight. Neither dive bomber was badly damaged.

The Battle of the Eastern Solomons was fought on 24 August, barely two weeks after the Marines first set foot on Guadalcanal. The Japanese intention was to sink or rout the remaining US Navy units in the Solomons and thereby isolate 'The Canal'. Once this was accomplished, the island could be recaptured with relative ease.

Eastern Solomons was an unequal match-up, pitting three Japanese carriers against two American. But in the $2\frac{1}{2}$ months since Midway, all US Navy torpedo squadrons had re-equipped with the TBF-1. It was a tremendous improvement over the situation which existed in early June.

However, the air groups of the carriers *Saratoga* and *Enterprise* were very much hodge-podge units. In the rush of events after Midway, squadrons had been put aboard ship with little thought to organisational matters. Those units which were operational and reasonably trained were needed immediately, and they were the ones which went to sea. Therefore, *Saratoga* operated her own dive bomber and scouting squadrons with a strange fighter unit and an orphaned torpedo squadron. This was the reorganised VT-8, related to the unfortunate *Hornet* sqadron in name only. The new skipper was Lt Harold H. Larsen, better known as 'Swede'.

Similarly, *Enterprise* retained only her own fighter and bomber units. The scout squadron was from the sunken *Yorktown* and — ironically — the torpedo squadron was officially *Saratoga's* VT-3. Like Torpedo 8, VT-3, was reorganised after Midway and had a new leader: Lt-Cdr Charles M. Jett. Both VT-3 and VT-8 had 15 TBF-1s.

On the afternoon of the 24th, *Enterprise*

Above: Allied airpower, vintage 1942. A TBF takes off from a South Pacific base which includes US Army B-17s and B-24s. / *Grumman*

Right: Shipboard photos were comparatively rare during most of 1942. But a photographer aboard USS *Saratoga* thought this incident worthy of recording. Ensign F. G. Herriman nosed up this TBF-1 of VT-8 on 16 September, incurring minor damage. / *R. M. Hill*

launched a 23-plane search mission which included seven of Lt-Cdr Jett's Torpedo 3 Avengers. Each was armed with two 500lb bombs. Widespread Japanese naval forces had been reported heading south towards Guadalcanal, and it was the search planes' mission to find and report them. *Saratoga's* mixed air group would be primarily responsible for the attack.

Nearly an hour and a half after launch, Lt-Cdr Jett and his wingman, Ensign R. J. Bye, made contact. Nearly 200 nautical miles north of their launch position, the two TBF pilots found a Japanese carrier. She was the 11,000 ton *Ryujo*, escorted by a cruiser and two destroyers.

Jett led Bye in a climbing circle to the northwest of the carrier, and the TBFs stalked their target for half an hour. At 1510 Jett and Bye commenced a horizontal bombing run on the carrier from 12,200ft, approaching from out of the sun. There was no anti-aircraft fire until both Avengers were nearly at the drop point. Their four bombs all landed close together less than 200ft from *Ryujo's* stern, causing what looked like one big splash. It was disappointing to come so close, but with the Japanese now alerted there was no point in staying. Zeros would surely be up to intercept, and Jett and Bye took a course for *Enterprise*. Theirs was the only horizontal bombing attack Avengers would make on a carrier.

At almost the same time, two more VT-3 pilots saw the *Ryujo* force. Lt J. N. Myers and Machinist H. L. Corl were in the next search sector when they sighted a lone enemy cruiser. They prepared for a bomb run but were suddenly intercepted by three Zeros. One passed so close to Myers that he could

Above: **A TBF squadron in vertical disposition high above billowy clouds, c1942.** / *Grumman*

see a wide red stripe around the fuselage. Though the enemy fighters scored no hits on their first pass, Myers and Corl were forced to break off and head for home. The cruiser was firing accurate AA bursts and one Zero pursued Corl's TBF into a cloud. Corl never returned, and was presumed shot down by the fighter. Myers' last glimpse took in the carrier force for the first time, following 10 miles behind the cruiser. Another pair of *Enterprise* search planes also found *Ryujo* at this time, but were chased off by the Japanese combat air patrol.

Meanwhile, the US carriers had been found. Within 25 miles of the task force, Myers was jumped by a Zero which shot up his TBF. In just one pass the Japanese pilot expertly put four 20mm shells and at least 50 7.7mm bullets into the TBF, wounding two of Myer's crew. When he made an emergency landing aboard *Saratoga*, Myers watched his plane pushed overboard. It was too badly damaged to repair.

Ensign Bye took on five Aichi 'Val' dive bombers. Firing his single .30cal nose gun, he damaged two before the unequal odds began to tell. When the Japanese began to gain an advantage, Bye wisely disengaged and sped from the scene. Though his TBF was unharmed, the strange dogfight had required too much fuel and Bye made a safe water landing. He and his crew were rescued by a US destroyer. Another of Lt-Cdr Jett's planes also succumbed to fuel exhaustion, but the crew was picked up by a PBY.

At 1430, an hour and a quarter after the *Enterprise* search was launched, *Saratoga* sent up 28 Dauntlesses and eight Avengers to strike *Ryujo*. Leading the VT-8 planes was Lt Bruce L. Harwood, who shortly had to turn back when his engine began to cut out. Among the remaining seven pilots was Ensign A. K. Earnest, sole surviving officer of the Torpedo 8 TBF detachment at Midway.

The *Saratoga* strike sighted *Ryujo* heading north at 15-20kts. The air group commander, H. D. Felt, decided to split his forces and try to sink the cruiser as well as the carrier. He ordered 21 SBDs and five TBFs after *Ryujo* and seven Dauntlesses with two Avengers to attack the cruiser *Tone*. Felt circled high overhead in his SBD, watching the attack develop.

Approaching from 12,000ft, the TBFs retained their altitude as long as possible in order to achieve maximum speed during the run-in. The Dauntlesses attacked almost immediately and smothered the carrier with smoke and spray from numerous near-misses. The target was so obscured that the five TBFs broke off three times during their approach, waiting for visibility to improve. Finally they reached a favourable position and initiated an 'anvil' attack; three attacking from *Ryujo's* starboard bow and two to port.

The big Grummans bored in at 200ft, indicating 200kts with their bomb bay doors open. All five launched their torpedoes between 800 and 900yds, and one of those dropped from starboard clearly scored a hit. Two others might have struck *Ryujo*, but results were uncertain. As the first TBFs pulled off the target, *Ryujo* was listing to starboard, burning badly.

Meanwhile, Cdr Felt saw the dive bombing attack had failed. None of the original SBDs assigned to the carrier had scored a hit. He therefore called the remaining Dauntlesses off the cruiser and redirected them against *Ryujo*. The SBDs heard this order but the two TBFs did not. Ensigns C. F. Morgan and R. A. Divine continued their torpedo attack against *Tone*, about three miles south, despite thick AA fire and the efforts of defending Zeros. Divine's Avenger was hit by machine gun fire but remained airborne. Though a 'certain' hit was claimed, *Tone* evaded both torpedoes, which were dropped off her starboard quarter.

Ryujo was not so fortunate. Felt and the remaining SBDs attacked and scored four direct hits with their bombs. This damage, added to the torpedo strike, proved fatal.

During retirement, Zeros jumped several *Saratoga* planes. Ensign E. R. Hanson turned his Avenger into four separate attacks, firing his .30cal each time. Accurate fire by the turret gunners also kept the Zeros at a respectful distance. Only two TBFs besides Divine's T-7 received any damage.

As the SBDs and TBFs headed home to *Saratoga*, *Ryujo* was already settling. Torpedo 8 had helped sink a carrier after all.

It had been a long, eventful day. But it was not yet done. Shortly before 1900 the US task force received warning of another Japanese air strike en route. Both carriers took immediate action to clear their decks. *Saratoga* launched her remaining planes — five TBFs and two SBDs — with orders to strike a battleship-cruiser formation reported to the north. The small attack group was led by VT-8 skipper Swede Larsen. Four of the Avengers found enemy cruisers and dropped torpedoes, but the fast ships dodged all four 'fish'. Two of the TBF pilots became disoriented in the gathering darkness and were forced to make water landings. One crew made its way to an island while the other took to life rafts.

Enterprise scrambled 15 Wildcats, nine Dauntlesses and seven Avengers. This impromptu strike had vague orders to look for another group of enemy ships reported in the vicinity of the former *Ryujo* contact. The F4Fs remained to defend the task force when Japanese aircraft appeared, but the SBDs and TBFs headed north. On the way, ARM3c C. L. Gibson in Machinist J. R. Baker's T-4 shot down a 'Val' dive bomber with two bursts from his turret gun.

Last pilot off *Enterprise* was the air group commander, Maxwell F. Leslie. He had led VB-3 at Midway and was now flying a TBF. He well recalls that 24th of August:
'I flew a specially configured TBF which had extra gasoline tanks for longer duration. It was considered the ideal type for CAGs to fly because it had good armament and extra radio equipment. This was a most interesting flight for me for several reasons. I was

Right: Leading the *Enterprise* Air Group during the Battle of the Eastern Solomons on 24 August, 1942 was Lt-Cdr Maxwell F. Leslie. A former dive bomber pilot, Leslie converted to an Avenger which he had fitted with a bomb bay fuel tank. This enabled him to fly a five-hour mission searching for a phantom enemy aircraft carrier. / *Leslie*

spotted aft for take-off because I required more run, and minutes before the take-off signal I was told to cut my engine. I didn't know the reason, but then I heard that a Japanese attack was imminent and the ship was manoeuvring.

'After a brief interval I was again told to start my engine and I took off. I made the usual left climbing turn and as I looked back I saw a puff of smoke come from the aft elevator where I had been parked. I later learned that a Jap bomb had made a direct hit, with the explosion killing several people below decks and the after elevator was blown up about two feet.

'I then departed on a track to catch up with the squadrons which were headed for what had been reported as an enemy carrier. At this instant I was approaching our AA screen of destroyers and the battleship *North Carolina*, and I happened to be looking at it when I saw several gun flashes which appeared to be shells coming in my direction. Sure enough, in another brief instant I noticed several small holes in my left wing. I dived for the water and got out of there as fast as 175kts would take me.

'I continued on the projected heading and attempted to contact the squadrons by radio, but no luck. I went to what was undoubtedly reported as the wake of fast ships, and it turned out to be a reef with the water breaking over it. The air group had departed *Enterprise* at about 1900 and it was now just before sundown and I visualised a difficult time locating the ship upon return well after dusk, and I was right. I never did contact my squadrons, and they had been ordered by *Enterprise* to head for and land at Guadalcanal.

'It was pitch dark when I arrived at the supposed area for *Enterprise* but all ships were running darkened and nothing was in sight. I then headed in what I thought was the proper course for the ships to retreat, and finally I passed over one which I could only observe because of the high-speed wake astern of it. I didn't know whether or not it was friendly, and they probably had the same concern about me. It was at least heading in the same direction as I, and that gave me some encouragement.

'After another half hour I received a plain language call over the radio saying, "Max keep coming and gain some altitude". It was my Annapolis classmate, Ham Dow, who was the radio officer on the staff of Admiral Fletcher, and it was the best news I had ever received. In those days radar wasn't too well developed, but Ham Dow was one of the most influential in developing it, and he stayed with my blip on the screen until I arrived in the task force area.

'It was now well after 2300, the ships were darkened and all I could see was their silhouettes on the water. I still didn't know if they were friendly or enemy. However, I then got the word via radio the *Saratoga* would turn on its running lights for me to land aboard. I had made but three or four carrier landings in a TBF and never one at night, but I was more than willing to try this one. It happened to turn out well.

'All planes on deck had been spotted forward getting ready for a sunrise launch, and they had been kept there until the last minute awaiting my arrival. I was told that in another five minutes they were going to have to be pushed aft, so that shows how narrow was the margin I had.

'I will forever have a profound debt of gratitude to the magic of radar and the persistence of Ham Dow in using it. I was quite deaf from the four and three-quarter hours in the air, but after Admiral Fletcher called me up to the bridge, he told me to go down to his cabin and turn in on his brass-railed double bed.'

So ended the TBF's first genuine carrier battle. The two torpedo squadrons had launched 27 planes in the course of four search-strikes, 20 armed with torpedoes. Twelve of these had attacked enemy ships, contributing to the sinking of the light carrier. The bomb-armed Avengers achieved no hits. Torpedo 8, which had suffered so heavily at Midway, lost two aircraft and one crew in this battle. Torpedo 3 lost five planes: one shot down, two ditched and two jettisoned.

Eastern Solomons gave the Navy its first accurate combat evaluation of the Avenger. The opinions and conclusions were largely summed up in VT-3's after-action report:

'It is considered that the TBF-1 has numerous possibilities as a combatant plane either as a scout, bomber, torpedo plane, inner and intermediate air patrol plane, and as a glide bomber. The possibilities of this plane are limited only by the experience and training of the individual combat crews. More armament is desirable to increase the defensive characteristics of the plane. With an increase in firepower, especially forward, this plane is considered superior in combat to Japanese dive bombers.

'There appears to be room for improvement in communication doctrine between an air group and its carrier, and between various air groups in a task force. Should the TBF-1 be used as a scout, it could effectively home an air attack group to a located enemy force. Minor arrangements of communication facilities in this plane will allow the radioman-turret gunner to key contact reports while manning the turret.

'The TBF-1 would be more effective as a

scout if it were equipped with a half-size belly tank (125-130gal capacity). Such an arrangement would allow the plane more endurance and still enable it to carry two 500lb bombs.'

Two further torpedo opportunities arose during the Guadalcanal campaign: the carrier Battle of Santa Cruz on 26 October and the two-day Naval Battle of Guadalcanal in mid-November.

Santa Cruz went badly for the US Navy. The carrier *Hornet* was sunk, and no Japanese combatants were lost, but the hard fought battle blunted Japan's next-to-last major drive against Guadalcanal. *Enterprise* operated the new Air Group 10 while short-lived *Hornet* temporarily flew a mixed air group which included VT-6. Only 10 torpedo-armed Avengers from these two squadrons found any targets, and the eight 'fish' they aimed at two Japanese cruisers all missed.

The climax of the Guadalcanal campaign came on 13 and 14 November. A major surface engagement in 'Ironbottom Sound' immediately north of the island was fought on the night of the 12th/13th. The Americans lost two light cruisers and four destroyers; the Japanese lost a pair of destroyers and left

Above: Torpedo Squadron 10 in echelon formation, with the air group commander's aircraft (marked GC) second in line. / *Grumman*

Right: A TBF-1 runs up in its parking area at a Solomons base, c1943. / *Grumman*

behind the crippled battleship *Hiei*. Unable to manoeuvre out of range, *Hiei* was subjected to a day-long series of air strikes throughout the 13th.

Three TBF squadrons operating from Henderson Field made a total of five attacks upon the Japanese dreadnought. Fifteen sorties were flown by Torpedo 10, six by VT-8 and 10 by the first Marine TBF unit, VMSB-131. From these sorties, 26 torpedoes were launched and 10 hits were scored. Battered, blazing *Hiei* finally sank that evening, the first enemy battleship sunk by US torpedo planes. The Avenger crews celebrated their success with mixed drinks of fruit juice and torpedo alcohol. And while Navy and Marine SBDs had contributed to the sinking, the TBF squadrons could claim the major share of the credit among the aviators.

Next day, 14 November, was equally frantic. In a bold daylight reinforcement effort, the Japanese sent nearly two dozen ships — transports escorted by destroyers — down the island chain towards Guadalcanal. A cruiser force was found in the same area by search planes, and was attacked by Navy and Marine aircraft. Torpedo 10 and VMSB-131 each contributed three Avengers to the strike, and they put four torpedoes into the 9,000 ton *Kinugasa*. As the TBFs pulled off the target, the heavy cruiser was burning fiercely, on her way to the bottom.

The Japanese transports were subjected to repeated, merciless air attack. Henderson Field was to have been knocked out by heavy shelling, but the much fought-over airstrip remained operational. In the final major US torpedo action of the campaign, VT-10 skipper Albert 'Scoofer' Coffin led seven VT-10 planes in a devastating attack on one column of transports. The *Enterprise* pilots scored three hits which sank two transports.

By the end of the day the Japanese effort was almost completely thwarted. Though nobody knew it at the time, the defeat of the reinforcement effort marked the final crisis which Americans would face at Guadalcanal. Another three months would pass before the island was secure, but the outcome was no longer so uncertain.

Secretary of the Navy James Forrestall later said that Grumman saved Guadalcanal. He was thinking mainly of the F4F Wildcat, and though the statement ignored the crucial contribution of the Douglas SBD, there was some merit to the assertion. For the Avenger had also made a contribution which outweighed its small numbers.

Below: **With advent of medium-sized Independence class carriers, Avengers found a new home. This TBF-1 of Composite Squadron 22 is landing aboard the name ship of the CVL class.** / *R. M. Hill*

Bottom: **Even smaller than the 10,000 ton Independence class light carriers were the numerous escort carriers, or CVEs. TBFs operated from these small flattops with relative ease, despite the restrictions of a 500-550ft flight deck. Auxiliary Scouting Squadron 26 was aboard USS *Charger* in 1942.** / *R. M. Hill*

Flying the Avenger

Rear-Admiral Hank Suerstedt

Hank Suerstedt flew in Composite Squadron 21 from October 1943 to July 1945, operating from the escort carriers *Marcus Island* and *Commencement Bay*. His combat experience in the TBF-TBM covered the Central Pacific campaign from the Palau Islands through the conclusion of the Philippine operation, during which he helped sink a Japanese midget submarine. Suerstedt continued flying the Avenger after World War II, finishing his association with the TBM as CO of Attack Squadron 213 in 1949. He retired from the Navy with the rank of rear-admiral.

Flight Characteristics

'The TBF-TBM was very heavy on the controls. It was flown by constant use of the elevator trim tab since the longitudinal aerodynamic forces were extremely difficult to physically overcome without the tab. I know other old TBF pilots who disagree with this assessment, however.

'I recall using the inside of both my knees routinely to control the lateral wing position of the aircraft. It was not normally desirable to change the aileron trim tabs since any change in the control force required was usually of a transient nature. Using leg force on the stick for lateral control worked quite satisfactorily.

'My primary concern was that if one did not lead the lowering of landing flaps with great forward throws of the trim tab wheel, the change in trim could send the airplane into a significant nose-up attitude.

'Carrier landings were not too difficult in TBFs or TBMs. After the "cut" by the LSO and dropping the aircraft nose, I always utilised my right hand and left wrist to pull the stick back forcefully in order to get the tail down for the wire engagement. Because the Casablanca class CVE (as I recall) had only six or seven arresting wires, and perhaps only five before barrier engagement, "diving

for the deck" was not frowned upon if it was done reasonably well. The pilots always considered it an easy out for the LSO to claim that this was the cause of an accident, and not the LSO's signals! What it did cause was an inordinate amount of TBF-TBM tyre blowouts. If a pilot consistently tried for the number two wire, as I did, the TBM landed on the after elevator which tilted the elevator forward and resulted in as much as a four to five-inch "curb" for the aircraft wheels to hit. There seemed to be far less recrimination and retribution for several blown tyres as compared to one barrier engagement!

'Aerodynamically, the TBM was an extremely predictable and honest aircraft, though somewhat cumbersome. When coming aboard in bad weather on a pitching deck, on a few occasions when slow and high at the "cut" once the nose dropped through, the aircraft required a momentary burst of full power in order to get the tail down. This kept the aircraft from dropping to the deck nose-down on the main landing gear, but it was most stimulating to roll to a stop, arrested by number two or three wire, and hear the air officer's "crash yodeller" still warbling and find yourself surrounded by the crash and rescue team.

Armament and Equipment

'The TBM-1C always seemed to have more firepower than the TBF-1. It may have been the psychological lift of two forward-firing .50cals, or it may have been that the TBM-1Cs were newer than the TBFs we flew in training, so they performed better. The TBM-3s were obviously better, though the APS-4 radar in a wing-mounted pod did not seem as reliable as the internal ASB radar with the old YAGI antenna and the A scope in the TBM-1 and -1C.

'The radio altimeter was so unreliable that on low-level night torpedo runs we put tape over the "traffic signal lights" (vertically arranged red, yellow, green) and flew using the exhaust reflection on the water. As a matter of practice for the same reason of reliability, I also taped over the artificial horizon at night and in IFR weather, and flew needle, ball, airspeed.

'The TBM-1C was designed to carry only 1,600lb of ordnance. We routinely carried four 500lb bombs and, as I recall, a Mark 13 torpedo weighed close to 2,000lb. That is perhaps why when going off a Casablanca class CVE (which could churn up 19kts on a good day) it was not too infrequent for a pilot to settle badly after launch, level off in the ground effect, and have to "pickle" off a bomb on "safe" when the detonating engine did not seem adequate to keep the Avenger airborne.

'The TBM-1C had rocket rails for the

Far left: Nobody made it aboard every time. A landing signal officer waves off a TBF from too high an approach. / *Grumman*

Left: Hank Suerstedt.

35

HVARs (High Velocity Aerial Rockets). They were adapted by the Naval Ordnance Test Station at China Lake and Cal Tech scientists from a British design. They consisted of a three-inch rocket motor in a body about five feet long and an interchangeable three-inch solid ogive head for ASW or a five-inch high explosive head. The ordinate was reasonably predictable and after some training plus combat experience, we were able to do fairly well with five-inch HE rockets against Japanese gun emplacement caves in the cliffs of the Palaus. We delivered them by making shallow dives, with zero deflection, directly at the gun caves (15ft by 20ft openings), firing and then rolling away in a high-G horizontal turn.

Anti-Submarine Warfare

'Unlike ASW-dedicated CVEs, we conducted ASW primarily for those ships in company with us or nearby and en route to an operation with us. We flew three types of Anti-Submarine Patrol (ASP), and about half of the deployment on *Marcus Island* was spent in ASW.

'Local ASP was flown around our own forces and consisted of what was known as a Love pattern, from the phonetic alphabet in use at the time. This turned out to be the most tedious. All of our ASP flights were usually about four hours long.

'Combat ASP was usually flown around task groups or ships within 50 or 60 miles of us, en route to the same objective. This was the most interesting. We flew cover for the CVEs, the logistic ships and transports on the way to the target area. It was during this phase, en route to the Mindoro and Luzon operations in December 1944 and January 1945, that the Japanese kamikaze aircraft started coming through in large numbers. Therefore, an FM-2 Wildcat frequently teamed with a TBM on CASP to protect the ship. It was also during this phase when, on the way to the Luzon invasion on 5 January 1945, I fatally damaged a midget sub off Cebu Island with depth chages while it apparently was manoeuvring for a torpedo shot at a cruiser. Reportedly the cruiser had General MacArthur's staff embarked. At any rate, the midget was sunk when rammed by a US destroyer. I was reluctant to use my three-inch solid ogive head HVARs on the sub for fear of hitting one of our own ships on a ricochet as they raced from all directions to get in on the kill!

'The third type of ASW patrol was flown in the objective area — the beach landing area during and after the landing. Generally, this was a barrier type of ASW patrol, flown by single aircraft for each open water area between islands off the landing beach or in sectors from geographical points near the target. This was generally about 10 miles off the beaches.

Bombing

'We found the TBM most accurate in steep glide bombing. This involved bringing the target along the nose, and when the target disappeared under the wingroot, rolling in from a split-S manoeuvre, so we were able to obtain about a 65° dive. As I recall, this gave us about 310kts using the propeller in low pitch as a brake, with the bomb bay open. Upon our return in March 1945 we found to our dismay that the TBM had been restricted to 20° or 25° dives because of wing-fold hinge failures! We routinely used 500lb, 1,000lb or 2,000lb bombs for this type of bombing.

'Because we used the Mark 5 depth charges on ASP flights with a non-safetying hydrostatic fuse, we could not return aboard ship with these charges. (Not many crews survived a water landing with these depth charges aboard.) At the invasion of Peleliu it was decided to use depth charges against land targets rather than dropping them at sea at the end of an ASP flight. With contact nose fuses they were extremely effective as a high concussion bomb against caves, especially in valleys and gun or trooop emplacements in areas of horseshoe shaped ridges. The concussion from these 250lb bombs was most impressive, even when seen from several thousand feet.

'We tried a little mast-head bombing, with limited success. We encountered the problem of incorrect fuse settings or some faulty fuses. This method of bomb delivery became very unpopular with the TBM crewmen after some aircraft returned riddled with shrapnel in the aft fuselage from their own 500lb bombs that had detonated on contact with the target.

Target Co-ordination

'Because I was too junior to lead large co-ordinated strikes and too senior to feel fulfilled as a follower, I voluntarily took all of the observation, target co-ordination, naval gunfire or artillery spotting flights available for the CVE task group, both in the Palaus and the Philippines.

'On target observation flights, we were routinely loaded with 10 100lb .001 delay-fused general purpose bombs, plus eight HVAR HE rockets. I would spot targets at low altitude primarily for reporting them for air strikes or for ship's guns. Of prime interest to me was the fact that I could save the optimum target for myself, for working over at the end of the period, which generally was most rewarding. Also of interest to me was that I could find prospective targets at low altitude; 100-150ft with little or no opposition. When I called in an air strike it usually resulted in great quantities of anti-aircraft fire and violent opposition from the Japanese. Following the strike, I could again go into the area at low altitude with no opposition from the ground. Trucks, tanks, boats, warehouses, supply stacks and an occasional camouflaged aircraft were the reward for this type of flight. The targets were frequently too small for a large air strike (20-plus aircraft) but most lucrative for a single aircraft. I carried an Army or Marine Corps artillery officer as spotter on all but naval gunfire flights.

Smoke Laying

'I carried a smoke tank in the bomb bay for two island invasions. The tank had an exhaust tail pipe which hung out of the after-end of the bomb bay. I vaguely recall that it was ram-air operated.

'The first time I carried a smoke tank was at Anguar Island in the Palaus. During a feint landing on the west side of the island to draw enemy troops away from the real landing on the opposite shore, another pilot and I smoked the beach ahead of waves of empty landing craft, making the mock landing. The second time was for the Luzon landings at Lingayan Gulf. There was a most impressive naval gunfire preparation, as well as pre-landing air strikes followed by aircraft smoking the beaches, all as the first landing waves approached the beach.

Supply Drops

'On a few occasions in the Philippines, it was required that we drop supplies to troops reportedly cut off from normal logistic means. Each TBM carried four parachute-retarded supply units. Each unit was about five feet long and about 24in in diameter. They contained water, rations, carbine ammunition and medical supplies, and were delivered "on call". The efficiency of this endeavour was never determined by us.

The Wright R-2600 Engine

'The engine, in retrospect, left something to be desired, and it sometimes delivered barely enough power after take-off to stay marginally airborne. This involved the routine heavy launch from a CVE, or an occasional incident such as pulling an unreleaseable gunnery banner through the main portion of Kennewick, Washington *and* their north-south phone lines. However, reliability on long flights seemed extremely good.

'There were such instances as rolling into a dive of 14,000ft with the prop in low pitch (as a brake in the dive) and high blower because of the altitude, and pulling out low on a high-speed recovery after massive enemy opposition, only to discover in great dismay that the engine was still at full throttle, low pitch (ie high prop RPM) with an astronomical amount of manifold pressure. Like 57in of mercury! The fact that the R-2600 held together and functioned after that, had to be a tribute to the engine design and the people responsible for it.

Crewmen

'They were, as a whole, outstanding. No doubt in World War II there was a small percentage of men who should have been doing something else, but the aircrew did all they were trained to do, and a lot more. The radioman who flew with me in VC-21 was even checked out in the remote control system originally intended as part of the Norden bombsight. He had only lateral control through the PPI (Pilot Position Indicator) but we practised to the point where we could engage it as we came off the target, after regaining level flight, and the radioman could find his way more or less back to the task group. We never thought he could do more than get us back in the general area if he had to, but it gave the crewmen some feeling that they had some control over their survival.

'I always insisted on a turret gunner who was also an aircraft mechanic. He not only could reassure me when the engine seemed to go into "automatic rough" at the 250-mile turn in a long search, but could also utilise his talents in other situations. Because of battle damage to the throttle linkage, I had to land at the marginally US-held airstrip on Peleliu. The only aircraft prior to mine was an SB2C which had spun in a day or so before trying to land with severe damage. My gunner/mechanic used his mechanical training to advantage by rapidly cannibalising the requisite parts from a nearby wrecked Betty and thus saved the day for us. We returned to the ship in good shape, being chased off Peleliu by a Japanese mortar.

'I feel obliged to say something for the TBF-TBM squadron torpedomen. These were the enlisted men responsible for the well-being and functioning of the aircraft torpedoes. The fact that we didn't see any aerial torpedoes from the time we commissioned in October 1943 until six or seven months later is not significant. The fact that we were in the states of Washington and Oregon where liquor rationing was extremely tight, and procurement limited, was significant. And most significant was the fact that many gallons of 180-proof torpedo alcohol turned into almost pure water at torpedo running time! However, with almost solid squadron backing, these crewmen survived professionally.'

View From the Turret

Charlie M. Westbrook

Charlie Westbrook enlisted in the Navy in 1942 and graduated from aviation mechanic school in May of 1943. Following aerial gunner and flight schools he joined Composite Squadron 10 late that same year, becoming an Aviation Machinist Mate Second Class. The squadron boarded the escort carrier *Gambier Bay* in early 1944, and remained aboard through the Marianas, Palaus, and Philippine campaigns. When *Gambier Bay* was sunk in the Battle of Leyte Gulf in October of 1944, Westbrook returned to the US and finished the war as aircrewman in a PBM flying boat squadron.

'Generally a gunner was an aviation mechanic or ordnance man. He got his training by first going through a trade school, next through gunnery school, then came flight training. He then went to a squadron for more of the same training as flight school. This usually took about one and a half to two years.

'I went to aviation mechanic school at Norman, Oklahoma, after three and a half weeks at boot camp. It was a three-school

Right: **Charles M. Westbrook.**

institute: metalsmith, ordnance and mechanics. I was taught the basics of airplane and engine mechanics. When I arrived, the school probably had 500 sailors. When I left, there were at least 30,000.

'Next I went to Purcell, Oklahoma, for four weeks of gunnery school. I won a case of beer for hitting 25 out of 25 skeet. Of course I cheated a little. I found a buddy who would get extra ammunition so that he and I could practise more than the others.

'From gunnery school I was sent to flight school in Florida. Here we were assigned to crews of three; pilot, radioman and gunner. At flight training our real responsibilities began. We learned to check the plane before flights for full gas tanks, oil, tyres, controls, and sometimes even to start the engine for a ground test. Also, the guns were inspected and ammunition loaded. This included the gunner's turret .50cal and the pilot's wing guns. The radioman took care of his radio and radar along with his .30cal.

'The training we had in Florida was torpedo runs with dummy warheads, dive and skip-bombing and gunnery flights. Another function was patrol. We carried live loads on these flights over the Atlantic, as German U-boats were still found occasionally.

'In November 1943, after one year in the Navy, I went to Seattle, Washington to join VC-10. The skipper was Lt-Cdr Ed Huxtable, and I still remember one of the first things he said. Mr Huxtable told us, "When you have the duty to fly, you had better be here and be sober!"

'At Astoria, Oregon, the flight training began again with some new manoeuvres: night bombing, firing at a towed target, etc. The aircrew flew with all the TBM pilots and began to have preferences with whom they flew. I remember hedge-hopping across the desert sand dunes near Holtville, California, with Ensign "Sandy" Sanderson, who barrel-rolled a TBM. It was very smooth, of course, because he had been a Douglas SBD dive-bomber pilot before coming to VC-10. But the roll was a "no-no" for TBMs.

'Another memorable flight was a night dive-bombing run to a target in the Salton

Sea. The night was very clear; I could see the target, but I had no perception of height for pull-out, so it was quite a thrill when we finally levelled out over the water.

'We moved to Brown Field at Chula Vista, California, south of San Diego, on 1 January 1944. From here VC-10 made three shakedown cruises aboard a training carrier. The first cruise aboard carrier was only for pilots, no air-crew. We crewmen went to North Island to get oriented for carrier procedure.

'I think it was at this time, in March, we were assigned to our regular pilots. I was with Ensign Hovey Seymour, the prewar Yale football star, and Larry Austin was radioman. On our second shake-down, the full crews were to fly. We went out to pick up the carrier south-west of San Clemente. Everything went fine on the approach until we were just aft of the ship and got the cut signal. At this time Mr Seymour gave it the throttle. We went past the carrier and up for 100ft or more. About this time the plane stalled out. It turned over on the port wing and fell off to the port side of the ship. We hit the water on the nose and port wing, the tail came back above the water for about 10sec, then sank.

'I was in the turret and got out after the plane went under, although the escape hatch was jammed at first. Larry Austin escaped through the door. I believe he had both ankles sprained from bracing his feet against the radio mounts. We never saw Mr Seymour again.

'The loss of Hovey Seymour had a sobering effect on the crew. He was our second operational loss since forming the squadron, after an F4F pilot was lost at the very beginning. But few of us knew the fighter pilot, so it had less effect.

'Next morning I caught a plane to North Island, then a bus back to Brown Field. There was a new pilot on the bus — Mr Seymour's replacement, Ensign Robert L. Crocker. I flew with him the rest of my time in VC-10. During one of our first talks he said to not hold back, but be sure to tell him if I didn't like the way our plane performed. After all, I was three or four years older, at age 25 or 26!

'The first combat operation for VC-10 and *Gambier Bay* was the invasion of Saipan in June 1944. During this time our crew was involved in a barrier crash when the tail hook missed the wire. Radioman Austin was injured when one of our wing guns went off while folding the wing. Mr Crocker and I flew without a radioman for some time after this.

'One day while on patrol north of Saipan we spotted a submarine in a rain squall. By the time we got to it, it had submerged. But we heard it was sunk the next day.

'We had another close call. Mr Sanderson and his crew were killed in a crash on take-off. Mr Crocker, Austin and I were in this plane ready to make the flight when we were relieved by Sanderson. We were scheduled for the next flight. Sanderson's gunner Bill Zanan and I had been together ever since mechanic's school.

'Then another TBM went in the water. While on patrol near Guam our plane, an old one, began losing power. We called the ship for relief. We were told to wait on station until relieved. Mr Crocker and I talked it over. My opinion was not to wait. We met our relief about halfway back to *Gambier Bay*. When we got to the carrier and started to land, of course the pilot put the propeller into low pitch. When he did, our plane began to drop. Mr Crocker jettisoned the bomb load, which probably saved us a dunking. We came around once more and made it in.

'The plane was inspected and since it checked out, it was assigned to the next crew. Lt(jg) Hank Pyzdrowski took it on the next flight and put it in the drink about one mile in front of the ship!

'At this time our supply base was in the Admiralty Islands. On our last stop at the Admiralties, there were literally hundreds of ships anchored in and out of the harbour. Cargo ships, troop transports, tankers, all loaded to the waterline. Though nothing was official, we knew the big one coming up was the return to the Philippines.

'In about a week we were on our way, and VC-10 flew anti-sub patrol. This remains one of the biggest thrills of my life: to fly over 750 ships in one armada, joined by another large convoy, all going to war.

'The morning we were surprised by the Japanese fleet off Samar, Mr Crocker and I were in the third TBM to leave the deck after the attack started. The radioman was a fill-in from another crew which didn't have a plane. We had only four rockets and our guns, but we pressed through what amounted to almost a dummy run in an attempt to divert the enemy ships from our force.

'Mr Crocker started a run on a cruiser, but it turned away so he shifted to a destroyer. He waited until his tracers were bouncing off the deck, then let fly with the rockets. I fired off a full can of ammo on the run. We didn't stick around after that. When we landed on a field south of Tacloban on Leyte, we found seven holes in the cowling and a 20mm hole in the port wing. But it really didn't matter. After we landed, a Wildcat came in on top of us and destroyed both planes. We got out without a scratch.'

The Cheap Seats

Captain William B. Chace

'The TBF offered its crewmen great rewards and some vexations which is, I guess, the prerogative of a big, beautiful babe — and that she was.

'The crew compartment, manned by two, consisted of the tunnel and an armoured turret with a .50cal above. The tunnel, encompassing about half the total airframe, was equipped with a bench seat (room for two), radio, radar, navigating board, and armament gear on a convenient forward bulkhead. Aft there was a .30cal "stinger" gun. Within this area an experienced crewman could create a crude but effective airborne CIC (combat information centre) to support his pilot and advance the mission. Whatever this mission might be: anti-sub patrol, glide bombing, night low-level attack, or interdiction of enemy airfields; the ability and response of this great aircraft was a challenge and a joy.

'The tunnel did not provide much comfort. It was a noisy enclosed capsule with very limited visibility. After days of intensive combat, it became encrusted with and smelled of engine oil and transmission fluids. There was no physical access to the cockpit, therefore it could produce a discouraging claustrophobia for the uninitiated.

'The advanced training held in Hawaii was to many a green crewman a first true revelation of his future "glamorous" role. Some of the more anxious types feigned airsickness as an out. One instructor on AirPac's staff had a standard treatment for the ailment. The vomiting patient was directed to the confined area in the tail where he could befoul only himself, and after landing he was made to thoroughly clean the compartment. If the performance was repeated, the man was indeed transferred out of flying. However, repeats were rare.

'In the summer of 1942 a radioman in Torpedo Squadron 6 died of carbon monoxide poisoning while in the landing circle waiting to board the *Saratoga*. This tragedy shook us all and generally caused pandemonium until it was determined that he had vented a small port in the tail designed to eject spent .30cal shell cases. Unfortunately, exhaust fumes had been

sucked into the tunnel rather than fresh air. When exhaustive investigation determined the cause, AlNav advices were heavily circulated, and I know of no other similar tragic instances.

'The problem of physical access in emergency was always a concern to pilot and crew. This also involved anxiety about failure of voice communications in the event of power loss. One pilot and radioman came up with a seemingly ingenious solution. The pilot's relief tube was extended down the tunnel where it was fitted with a funnel, thus creating a crude gosport. A flip of the wings initiated a gosport drill. All went well until a long anti-sub patrol the pilot absent mindedly sought to use his relief tube for its originally intended purpose, and the irate radioman got the wet end. The rest of us belayed plans for similar installations.

'As I can personally attest, the relative spaciousness and general configuration of the tunnel mandated that loose gear be well secured during take-off and landing. On the squally, black night of 25 January 1944, Task Force 58 was making a fast run in to support initial landings at Kwajalein. Among the force was *Enterprise*, whose mission was to launch a predawn fighter sweep to interdict the enemy airbase of Taroa on Maloelap atoll.

'As zero hour approached, it became apparent that with almost no visibility, launching would be difficult and rendezvous of the Hellcats nearly impossible. It was decided that Air Group Commander Roscoe Newman would be launched first in a radar-equipped TBF to serve as a reference point for the F6Fs over a guide destroyer. I would be observer at radar in the tunnel.

'It was a catapult launch. Since radar was the name of the game that night, electronics technicians were swarming about the plane until we were locked on to the catapult. The engine revved, the launch signal flashed.

'Somewhat later I heard a distant voice in my earphone. "Pilot to radar, where are you?" After a few repeats of this, I came to and responded. One of the technicians had left a black box loose atop the radar, and it had zocked me right between the eyes on take-off. Under nearly impossible visibility conditions,

Commander Newman assisted a partial rendezvous and vector for 15 or so Hellcats. Taroa ceased to be a threat and Kwajalein is history. Back on deck he questioned my early lack of response. I could think of no better reply than a diffident, "a little electronic trouble, sir."

'Several years after World War II, while cruising along the coast of Maine, my wife and I were asked to visit the summer home of a Grumman design engineer. He and I established our mutual interest in the TBF. Unfortunately, it wasn't the time or place to pursue the subject, but I did ask how it was that the confining turret was so remarkably comfortable over long patrols and missions. He smiled and, pointing, said, "There's the prototype."

'Stashed in a corner of the farmhouse ell was the post and saddle seat of an old-horse-drawn hay rake. It seems fitting that this seat, that had for years eased Yankee farmers over fields looking down the blue waters of Eggomoggin Reach, should have equally eased latter-day Yankees on far-flung missions in the Avenger.'

Left: Bombardier's station looking forward, where most of the radio equipment was located. The ordnance arming panel is on the left side of the transverse bulkhead, next to a console containing an altimeter and skid indicator. The latter two instruments were necessary for a bombardier. At top centre is the lower portion of the gunner's turret.
/ Grumman

Below left: The TBF-1 bombardier's station looking aft. Later the radioman occupied this position by himself, when the heavy Norden bombsight-autopilot system was discarded.
/ Grumman

Plane Captain

Michael J. O'Malley

'Keep 'em flying' became a popular phrase during World War II. But the men who were responsible for this crucial job seldom receive the credit and appreciation they deserve. In an attempt to help correct this lamentable condition, perhaps the recollections of one plane captain (as the Navy called its crew chiefs) may serve as a tribute to all.

Mike O'Malley was an Aviation Machinist Mate Second Class with Torpedo Squadron 11 at Henderson Field, Guadalcanal, during 1943. As plane captain of the TBF-1 marked T-5, O'Malley was responsible for keeping that Avenger operational. The regularly assigned pilot of T-5 was Lt (jg) George H. Gay — formerly Ensign Gay of Torpedo 8.

Below: Michael J. O'Malley, VT-11 plane captain on Guadalcanal in 1943. O'Malley kept the TBF of Lt(jg) George Gay operational — the same Ensign Gay who was the sole survivor of *Hornet's* VT-8 TBDs at Midway. Barely visible on the cowling is the aircraft name, *Fish Eyes.* / O'Malley

'The TBF was a fine aircraft to work on. It did the job and delivered the payload. Its weaknesses were seldom noticed — only cockpit errors or maintenance discrepancies caused some losses, not counting enemy action. The TBF took a lot of punishment and kept on flying.

'A plane captain's duties were many:
1 Maintaining your assigned aircraft in tip-top condition at all times.
2 Assisting others in periodic maintenance checks; 30, 60 and 90-hour inspections.
3 Assisting instrument, ordnance or radio people with the aircraft.
4 Taxying or transporting aircraft for modifications or transfer.
5 Briefing new or unassigned pilots on various aspects of your aircraft's peculiarities.

'Daily inspections were performed, and began with a complete walk-around visual inspection. This usually began at the propeller, which was inspected for nicks, dents, cracks and rough edges. Mental notes were made for further action if necessary. Then the propeller was pulled through about 12 blades. Naturally, the cockpit was checked prior to this for any switches left on.

'Next was the engine cowling, looking for popped rivets, dents, cracks, unusual metal stresses or discolouration from heat or foreign objects. While inspecting the cowling, the engine front cylinders were checked for loose spark plug leads, cylinder cooling fins for chips or cracks, discolouration or leakage of oil at the base and rocker arm covers. The prop controls were inspected for looseness and security of hold-down nuts and fraying of control cables and pulleys. Other components of the front cylinders and nose section were gone over by feel.

'The plane captain examined the exhaust system in accordance with daily pre-flight inspections. So was the rest of the aircraft: landing gear, oleo struts, tyres, wheels and wheel wells. All wing surfaces and tail surfaces, both metal and fabric areas. Then on to the fuselage, greenhouse, bomb bay doors, plexiglass and gun bays. All external controls were examined and moved in their proper directions and limitations for freedom of movement. Wing lights, tail light, recognition lights, formation lights and lenses were gone over as well as the landing lights.

'Once the plane captain was satisfied and had a good mental picture of his aircraft, he ventured further into interior areas requiring daily checks. Upon completion of the radio and turret bays, he climbed into the cockpit, gave it the once-over, and began signing off some of his daily preflight check list, usually called the Yellow Sheet. Any mental notes gathered on the visual walk-around were noted here, if worthy of mention to the pilot or maintenance crew.

'At this time (1942-43) we never had ground power units to assist in starting the R-2600 Wright Cyclone engine. We had hand-cranked inertia starters, and while one man was setting the mixture control and throttle for starting, the poor devil on that hand crank sure took a beating. It was his duty to gain speed as he cranked, and at the right moment he pulled out his crank and gave a thumbs-up gesture. The plane captain switched on his magnetos, depressed his brakes, waited for the first cough of the engine, and slowly advanced the mixture control to provide fuel as the engine began to grab hold. Soon the throttle and mixture were in proper position for run-up. Instruments were checked; fuel and oil pressure up in the green, hydraulic pumps and generator and other accessories in the green. The power plant was run at a pre-described setting while the engine warmed up to operating temperature.

'Meanwhile, all controls were exercised. Flaps, rudder, ailerons, elevator, bomb bay doors, wing locking mechanisms, canopy and seat, brake and rudder pedals. All safety switches were checked for correct placement of brass safety wire. Loose gear such as maps was stowed away.

'I believe the critical area on the R-2600 was around 1,100rpm, so one quickly passed that reading when the propeller was to be cycled, up to around 1,300, and the prop control was moved from high pitch to low pitch. This allowed the oil in the prop dome to replenish and receive warm oil to the cam track and mechanisms for smoother prop performance. The final engine check was to advance the throttle to max, hold her a few seconds and check the rear bank of spark plugs and then the front bank by turning the magneto switch to left and to right. At this time we were allowed a 100rpm mag drop. If after several run-ups we were unable to burn out the mag drop, it usually meant a plug change and timing of the mags.

'After letting the engine temperature settle down to a normal reading, the engine was shut down and the yellow sheet signed off for engine operational check.

'Once again a cockpit check was made: all instruments back to normal settings, no unusual smells or odours indicating gas, oil, hydraulic fluid, burnt wiring or the like. Back outside to the engine and a visual check for oil seepage or fuel stains. Once satisfied that the aircraft was ready, a thumbs-up gesture was given to the line chief as he passed by. Any remaining time left was used in cleaning the aircraft and preparing to receive the pilot.

'As the pilot approached the aircraft, one usually went out a few steps and met him and began to "sell" the aircraft. He performed a walk-around, all the while the plane captain standing one foot to the right and rear, watching every action. If a question was asked, it was promptly answered, or had better be! If the pilot was satisfied, he climbed into the cockpit, where the plane captain aided him with the shoulder harness. Finally, a few words on the particular aircraft because very few are ever exactly the same in performance, fuel consumption or flight attitude. Then the yellow sheet was presented to the pilot, and upon his signature the plane captain was "bailed out" because if that aircraft failed to return for some mechanical reason, the pilot had assumed full responsibility.

'Upon landing, the plane captain received the aircraft and through various taxi signals brought it to a parking area, chocked the wheels and climbed to the cockpit. There he assisted the pilot in removal of shoulder harness and received mechanical performance or malfunction information. The squadron flight officer needed to know if the aircraft was ready for another mission.

'The post-flight inspection once again involved a complete tour of the previous checks made on the preflight, except for engine run-up. The aircraft was then refuelled, any oil stains wiped away, and the line chief was given a thumbs-up for aircraft in a ready for flight posture. Wheel covers were installed, landing gear locks inserted, tail surfaces locked and battened down, pitot tube cover installed, propeller aligned, cowl flaps closed, carburettor heat door closed, bomb bay doors closed, canopy shut, and your torpedo plane was secured.'

The Leatherneck Contribution

Lester T. Ludwig

Over 20 US Marine Corps squadrons carried the VMTB designation during World War II, identifying them as TBF or TBM units. Half of them never reached combat, either being assigned permanent training duties or being involved in training when the war ended. A few Marine Avenger squadrons flew from escort carriers before the war ended, but the bulk of 'Leatherneck' TBF-TBM units were land-based. Representative of the men who served with these squadrons was Les Ludwig.

'I graduated from Fall City, Washington, High School, in May 1943 and joined the Marine Corps in June. I was sent to San Diego, California, for basic training and upon completion of basic I was transferred to the USMC Air Base at El Centro, California, where I completed gunnery school. This training included radio and radar operations and procedures, and maintenance and use of .30 and .50cal air-cooled machine guns.

'We trained in the SNJ trainer with swivel twin .30cal machine guns. The training included firing at targets being towed by other aircraft in flight, hours of trap and skeet shooting, and ground firing with .30 and .50cal at moving targets. We also fired from fixed turrets on the trap range with "birds" being thrown at us from fixed positions.

'After graduation from gunnery school I was assigned to VMTB-242. The squadron had been overseas during the Guadalcanal campaign and returned to the States for a rest and regrouping. It consisted of 50 pilots and 100 gunners (50 radio and 50 turret). The commanding officer was Maj William W. Dean. I was asked to be the turret gunner for 1-Lt G. H. "Tiny" Thompson. Fred Priestman from New York was the radioman.

'The squadron returned overseas in

Above: **Lester T. Ludwig.**
/ Ludwig

Left: **Marine Avengers formed a major part of Solomons Strike Command. Here are TBFs and SBDs at Munda in October 1943.** */ R. M. Hill*

Above: The diamond insignia on the tail identified this TBM-3 as belonging to VMTB-232, flying ground support missions at Okinawa in June 1945.
/ R. M. Hill

Below: By January 1944 the New Georgia group was serving Allied aircraft on a large scale. This TBF-1 taxies to the flight line on Vella Lavella.
/ R. M. Hill

Top: **A trio of VMTB-232 Avengers over Okinawa. This squadron saw extensive service throughout the war. Originally VMSB-232, it was destroyed on the ground at Pearl Harbor, then became the first dive bomber unit at Guadalcanal. It also participated in the latter Solomons campaign, then moved through the Central Pacific until flying into Kadena Airfield, Okinawa, in April 1945. /** *R. M. Hill*

January 1944. We arrived at Espiritu Santo in the New Hebrides for more training. The squadron was then sent to Bougainville for strikes against Japanese-held islands to the north and west. The main island and airstrip we hit was Rabaul, New Britain. The Japanese held most of the islands in that area, but they were cut off from most supply lines.

'The main problem on Bougainville was the continual shelling of the airstrip at night. Just after dark the shells would start falling. It was thought that the Japs had some large artillery on rails that were under cover and at night they would roll them out, drop a few shells, and move back under cover. On

several occasions, planes from 242 would leave in the morning trying to locate the guns, but without success.

'The main duty of the TBF turret gunner on any strike was protection of the aircraft from enemy planes approaching from the rear. Also, after the pilot dropped the bombs we would go in on a strafing attack of buildings, planes, etc, from low altitude.

'The turret was equipped with a single .50cal machine gun which was fed from the underside by a can holding the belt of ammunition. When this can was empty we could pull a pin, dropping the can, and the radioman pushed another full can up into the gun. The .50cal was on the left side of the

gunner, shoulder high. In front was a pistol grip used for control of the turret and trigger for the gun, with bullet-proof glass in front of the gunner. The turret gunner had to climb up into the seat and pull the armour plate up underneath him. He was well protected except from the top and right side of the turret. The gun controls had automatic shut-off switches so the tail or wing-tip wouldn't be hit when we were firing. However, these didn't always work. One pilot thought they worked all the time and told his gunner to try it. The gunner shot off the wing-tip.

'The strikes over Rabaul were mainly on the airstrips. However, at times the town was hit with incendiary bombs. Our squadron would leave Bougainville with a squadron of SBDs and fighter escorts. The dive bombers were the first in, trying to knock out the anti-aircraft guns. Then we would attack from three directions in what was called a glide bomb run, drop the bombs, and leave as quickly as possible. The glide would start from 10,000 to 15,000ft. We would drop our bombs at about 1,500ft, then descend to the treetops and move out. This was when the turret gunner would start his strafing.

'I experienced two crash landings, with no injuries. The crash landing on Bougainville was due to heavy AA fire over the town of Rabaul. The plane was shot up badly from an almost direct hit underneath. We made it back to Bougainville and brought the plane in. I received one small piece of flak in my left shoulder and a small calibre bullet went through my water canteen without hitting me.

'From Bougainville we were sent to Sydney, Australia, for a week of rest. Then we returned to the New Hebrides and were sent to Pearl Harbor for more training in anti-submarine patrol. After returning to the

South Pacific, our new TBMs were equipped with depth charges and rockets. Our squadron was then sent to the Marianas and helped the Marine ground forces by flying from the island of Tinian. We also began anti-sub patrol missions.

'When the ships left the Marianas for Iwo Jima, VMTB-242 was on standby for the flight north. It was planned that when the invasion started, the south beach would be taken and the airstrip secured so our squadron could land on Iwo Jima. In March 1945 notification came that the Marines had landed on the south beach and were working north. This was the clue for us to take-off.

'We had just enough gas to fly from Tinian to Iwo Jima (about 800 miles) and if the airfield wasn't secured we would have to land on an aircraft carrier lying offshore. When we approached Iwo Jima all we could see was smoke and dust. While flying over the island I called our pilot and asked him where the airstrip was because everything looked the same — all torn up. We did manage to land between the shell holes and refuel and load up with bombs which had been brought up from the beach. We flew ground support for the front lines until the island was secured. We then started anti-sub patrols again, until our return to Tinian in the Marianas.

'At this time the squadron was put on notice to be ready to leave again — rumour said Formosa — but another squadron relieved us and VMTB-242 returned to the States.

'The TBF and TBM were sometimes called "flying coffins" but we aircrews felt they were the safest plane flying. The large engine was dependable, and the large bomb bay withstood water and crash landings very well. My second crash landing was at Iwo Jima, and fortunately there were again no injuries.'

Choose Your Weapons

The Avenger carried a more diverse armament than any other carrier aircraft of World War II. Besides .30 and .50cal machine guns and conventional bombs or torpedoes, it also employed depth charges, acoustic homing torpedoes, air-to-surface rockets and even aerial mines. In short, there was no form of strike mission for which the Avenger was unsuited.

The large majority of Avenger sorties were flown with bombs rather than torpedoes. This was a factor of mislearned lessons in the Pacific and the nature of the war in the Atlantic. In the Pacific, Japanese warships were seldom encountered at sea after 1942, and TBFs and TBMs were therefore employed more often against ground targets. Even when enemy shipping was attacked, erroneous conclusions drawn as a result of the disastrous Midway torpedo attacks led to Avengers being armed mainly with bombs. Not till after the First Battle of the Philippine Sea in June 1944 did Avengers return largely to torpedoes as their proper naval strike weapon. But even then, disappointment resulted due to still-faulty torpedoes.

In the Atlantic, where Axis shipping was virtually non-existent, conventional aerial torpedoes were almost never carried. Gravity bombs or, more often, depth charges were the standard armament. However, after the homing torpedo was available and its special anti-submarine qualities recognised, sub-hunting Avengers were frequently armed with 'Fidos', of which more later.

The Avenger's maximum bomb load was rated at 2,000lb in varying combinations. All were carried on shackles within the large enclosed bomb bay and the most frequent loading was four 500lb General Purpose bombs. These could be dropped singly, in pairs, or in salvo, depending upon the tactical situation. Their fusings were varied on most strike missions in order to achieve a variety of damage. Instantaneous fusing would detonate the bomb on contact, while delay settings such as 1/100 or 1/250 of a second would allow the bombs to penetrate buildings and thin-hulled vessels to explode inside. Attacks on enemy airfields and other land facilities frequently used delayed-action fuses which set the bomb 'cooking' for

Below: A fully-loaded TBM-1C with four High Velocity Aerial Rockets under each wing. Note also the radar antenna below the port wing and gun cameras mounted before the cockpit, aft of the radioman's position, and under the wing. The white ball on the vertical stabiliser identified the Avenger as belonging to USS *Hornet,* namesake of the carrier sunk in 1942. / *IWM*

several hours after the raid was over. This had the advantage of prolonging the effect of the raid and of inhibiting repair parties. Delayed-action 1,000lb bombs were particularly effective in this role.

When Avengers salvoed their entire load at once, usually employing four 500lb GPs, an intervalometer determined the spread. This was an electric solenoid which could be set to give a wide or tight pattern, depending upon the effects desired. It was based on the planned airspeed and release altitude the pilot was instructed to employ against a specific target. Therefore, the pilot lined up his target at the briefed speed and altitude, and pressed the button on his stick which dropped his load. The solenoid controlled the interval of each bomb's release automatically. There were instances of 'hung bombs' when the intervalometer failed to release one or two bombs, but by and large it was an effective procedure.

As TBFs and TBMs were frequently employed in ground support for amphibious troops, a variety of lighter bombs were also available. For use against enemy personnel or positions, either 10 100lb or four 250lb bombs were common. These were fragmentation bombs, also known as 'daisy cutters' since they could be fused to explode slightly above ground level and spread shrapnel in all directions. Such weapons were also effective against exposed anti-aircraft guns.

Originally the Avenger was to have employed a high-level bombing technique with the Norden bombsight and its Stabilised Bombing Approach Equipment. In fact, it was seldom used and was widely

Above: Two 500lb bombs in the bomb bay of the XTBF-1. A full load amounted to 2,000lb of ordnance, either bombs or a torpedo. / *Grumman*

Right: A Marine Corps ordnance crew pushes what appears to be a 1,000lb bomb under a TBF 'somewhere in the Pacific'. The lack of many facilities is apparent: no steel mat for the parking area, the rocks improvised as wheel chocks, and no sign of a tractor to haul the heavy bombs to their planes. / *Grumman*

disliked by aircrews because of its weight. Flying straight and level at 7,000-15,000ft and hoping to hit a fast, wildly manoeuvring warship was to engage in fruitless optimism. Early combat experience during the Guadalcanal campaign in late 1942 proved the hopelessness of this technique. But due to the bureaucratic inertia which dogs all well-organised endeavours, including total war, the Norden system remained a standard piece of Avenger equipment until well into 1944. Its only regular use was engagement of the SBAE as an auto-pilot on lengthy searches or patrols.

TBFs and TBMs were much more profitably employed in the technique known as glide bombing. A shallow, low attack made at moderately fast airspeed offered better chances of scoring a telling hit on any target, and as experience and tactics evolved, this was the technique most widely used. It was first employed by the reorganised Torpedo Squadron 6 aboard *Enterprise* in July 1942, immediately after the Battle of Midway. The squadron had been all but annihilated in its Douglas TBDs, and the new pilots set about experimenting with their brand new Grummans. They found that attacking in a steep glide from 6,500ft and releasing their bombs at 2,500ft resulted in all bombs within 40ft of a moving target. It was exceptional accuracy.

However, there were new problems. The prolonged glide runs generated excessive stresses on the airframes, and structural failures occurred. Additionally, because the TBF did not have a bomb displacing gear as did the Douglas SBD dive bomber, in the steepest approaches some bombs struck the Avengers' fuselages as they were released. The latter problem was cured by limiting the dive angle to 60°, but strengthening the airframe beyond all chance of failure would have added about 500lb. This was clearly unacceptable, and as a compromise Grumman installed heftier parts in the affected portions of the airframe.

Pressing glide bombing attacks down to only 2,500ft brought Avengers well within range of light-calibre automatic weapons. Therefore, in an effort to provide pilots with more effective flak suppression, the single forward-firing .30cal machine gun was replaced by two .50cals in the wings. This modification first appeared in the TBF-1C in 1943, plus additional armour and provision for underwing drop tanks.

Torpedo attack, in theory if not in practice, remained the Avenger's primary mission. A 2,100lb torpedo could be carried in the bomb bay, and while the early wartime US torpedoes were woefully ineffective, at least the TBF's vastly improved performance over the TBD allowed adoption of new tactics.

Instead of the customary low, straight-in

Left: This photo was probably taken at Henderson Field, Guadalcanal, in late 1942 or early 1943. Note the pierced steel planking, dirt revetment, and bearded ordnanceman standing by to winch the bombs into place. / *Grumman*

Below left: Hoisting bombs into an Avenger aboard a fast carrier, c1944. Notice the distinctive folding mechanism of the bomb bay doors. / *Grumman*

Below: Clusters of incendiary bombs are assembled by ordnancemen aboard a fleet carrier during strikes against Tarawa Atoll in September 1943. / *Grumman*

approach which hampered manoeuvrability and restricted airspeed, tactics evolved by VT-3 in late 1941 helped offset some of the Devastator's limitations. The torpedo pilots found that by approaching the target ship at higher altitude they gained three major advantages. They had better visibility, the dive towards the drop point increased speed and helped shorten exposure to AA fire, and escorting fighters could better protect the torpedo planes and dive bombers simultaneously. The TBF-1, with its 60mph speed advantage over the TBD, capitalised upon these new procedures. However, the

Avenger's full potential as a torpedo plane was not realised until new 'fish' arrived in 1943 which could be dropped from more than 100ft.

Ideally, a torpedo attack was co-ordinated with dive bombers in order to split the enemy's defences and thereby increase the effectiveness of the torpedo planes and also to cover their vulnerable withdrawal. When attacking fast warships such as aircraft carriers or cruisers, the Avengers attempted to gain a drop position 800-1,000yds off each bow. Then if the target turned towards one set of torpedoes in order to present the

Top and above: **The progress of an aerial torpedo attack. As the first TBF looses its torpedo, following planes continue their run. Then, as the leading Avengers bank away, the others also make their drops. Ideally, an entire squadron followed this procedure by attacking an enemy ship from both bows in an 'anvil' attack.** / *Grumman*

narrowest view, it was broadside to the second spread.

Avengers participated in the destruction of six Japanese aircraft carriers, but only two were sunk entirely or largely by torpedoes. Three battleships and 14 cuisers also were sent to the bottom in whole or in part by TBFs and TBMs, both with bombs and torpedoes. These figures do not include another dozen major warships which were attacked by Avengers (in company with other aircraft) and sunk or destroyed while in dockyard at Kure Harbor in July and August 1945. These 'sitting ducks' — six carriers, three battleships and three cruisers — were mostly immobile, and their destruction gives little demonstration of the Avenger's

capabilities against capital ships manoeuvring in open water.

The VT squadrons finally obtained an effective aerial torpedo in 1944, but not without difficulty. The skipper of VT-13, Lt-Cdr Larry French, recalls the event:

'The "ring-tail" torpedo was designed and developed by the California Institute of Technology, modifying the standard Mark 13-1A aerial torpedo with a steel band about 10in wide which was wrapped and welded around the tail fins. This ring-tail stabilised the torpedo in flight and protected the steering mechanism on contact with the water. There were probably some internal modifications as well.

'Cal Tech tested these torpedoes by using

an old log chute to launch them into a lake. Thus you can see it was most difficult to get the Navy interested and to make an aerial test. But I believe VT-13 was the first squadron in the fleet which had the ring-tail. In early 1944 while USS *Franklin* was in San Diego, I was called by the captain to attend an AirPac conference regarding the flight testing of this torpedo.

'We loaded 16 VT-13 planes at North Island with the ring-tail and the *Franklin* was the target off Point Loma. The torpedoes had dummy warheads, and depth regulators were set to pass under the carrier. The 16 torpedo planes attacked the carrier from ahead and 30°-45° on port and starboard bows, simultaneously. They were launched at 500-800ft altitude at speeds of 240-280kts (275-325mph). The altitude and airspeed varied in order to gain proper entry angle into the water. All the ring-tails appeared to run hot, straight and normal, with many "hits" reported by lookouts on the *Franklin*.

'Our tests showed the the ring-tails could be launched at airspeeds up to 280kts and altitudes as high as 800ft. The only restriction was that the plane had to be in straight and level flight at time of release.

'However, there were only about 56 such torpedoes in the programme at that time. The *Franklin* and I wanted all these torpedoes put aboard, as we were sailing to the war zone. But due to continuation of evaluation and testing, we got 48.

'The first use of these ring-tails was 4 August 1944 against a Japanese convoy of six transports with nine destroyer types escorting. Before launch, our admiral told me, "I do not want to include in my action report some shipping damaged... I want them sunk!"

'Air Group 13 attacked this convoy about 70 miles west of Iwo Jima. Our strike included 12 Hellcat fighters to strafe and suppress AA fire, 30 SB2C dive bombers, and

my 16 TBMs. The bombers attacked first and scored no direct hits. As the last VB pulled away the guns ceased firing and all seemed quiet. Then suddenly it happened. I couldn't believe it! The convoy made a 45° port turn towards us. I immediately ordered, "Attack, attack, attack." Before launch I had briefed the squadron that each four-plane division would concentrate on one ship each for sure kills. However, due to the sudden attack situation, some pilots in the last division veered off and took shots at the two other ships.

'We dived down over the left side of the screen and broke through the AA fire. We were inside the screen, approaching the torpedo release point at 220-240kts at 400ft. Of course, the convoy opened fire with everything it had, but it was too late. We all came through the AA fire, had great torpedo shots at the transports at very short range.

'VT-13 claimed the sinking of all six transports. This was confirmed by the air group commander, and later by surface ships sent to investigate the area. It is my firm belief that had VT-13 used the regular aerial torpedo, dropping at 100-110kts at 100ft, we could not have successfully made this attack, as our losses would have been excessive. But we lost no planes or crews, and had had heavy damage to one TBM and light damage to three others. From then on we used the ring-tails in the Sibuyan Sea and other Philippine areas.'

Another type of torpedo became available in 1943, the year which might be considered the rennaissance of naval air ordnance. This was

Above: The nine pilots of VT-13 who sank six Japanese transport ships near the Bonin Islands on 4 August 1944. This was the first combat use of the ring-tail torpedo. / *French*

Below left: Cdr Larry French, skipper of VT-13 aboard USS *Franklin* in 1944, who led successful anti-shipping strikes with new ring-tail torpedoes. / *French*

Above: A TBM-1 of Composite Squadron 80 off USS *Sargent Bay,* showing the full-length British style rocket rails under each wing. / *R. M. Hill*

the acoustical 'Fido' anti-submarine weapon, so named because it followed its target not unlike a pet dog by homing in on a submerged submarine's engine noise. Fido and a new 500lb depth bomb became instrumental in the U-Boat campaign of the Atlantic during 1943, and that year accounted for nearly two dozen sinkings between them. Like conventional bombs, the depth charge could be released in singles, pairs, or salvos, depending upon the pattern desired.

Undoubtedly the most spectacular new weapon was the five-inch High Velocity Aerial Rocket which was issued to composite squadrons in the Atlantic at the end of 1943. Early US Army Air Force 'bazooka' type launchers were tested for possible Navy use in the spring of that year, but their low velocity and the weight of the tubular launcher were deemed unsuitable. That summer a British rocket was tested on Avengers, using a rail-type launcher. But shortly the US Navy's Bureau of Ordnance and California Institute of Technology came up with the HVAR, fired from 'zero-length'

rails which reduced weight. TBM-3s came from the factory with zero-length rails and radar sets as standard equipment, which made them ideal for anti-submarine work. The rockets were issued to operational squadrons in December and were first employed in combat by Avengers from the escort carrier *Block Island* in January 1944, on U-Boat patrol in the Atlantic.

The HVARs were an immediate success. With three or four under each wing, they gave an Avenger more than the broadside of a destroyer. Their superior range and penetration made them ideally suited for attacking heavily armed U-Boats, as the attack did not have to be pressed nearly as close as a bomb run. Fired singly or in pairs, HVARs had an effective range of over 400yd. In the Pacific they proved effective against shipping and heavily reinforced structures such as hangars, bunkers, and flak emplacements. One exuberant Avenger pilot, after first trying rockets against Japanese-held island targets, proclaimed them 'the greatest thing since the nickel cigar'.

HVARs were frequently loaded in TBMs

58

Above: **This exceptionally clear shot demonstrates the 'zero-length' rocket rails of a VC-84 TBM-3 from USS *Makin Island*. / *R. M. Hill***

with reduced bomb loads aboard escort carriers. Weight was always an important consideration in getting off the short deck of a CVE, and therefore a normal Avenger armament would be eight HVARs and two 500lb GPs.

Aerial mines were employed by Avengers only once on a large scale. This occurred during a fast carrier strike by Task Force 58 against the Palau Islands at the end of March 1944. The TBFs of Torpedo Squadron 2, 8 and 16 laid their mines close to shore in order to bottle up numerous Japanese ships and prevent them from leaving the anchorage. But it was risky business, as the Avengers had to fly low, predictable patterns well within range of shore-based AA guns. Subsequently, mine sowing was done mainly by long-range patrol planes or USAAF heavy bombers.

Not all Avenger equipment was limited to ordnance. There were other devices which aided the employment of weapons against specialised targets, particularly in the continuing anti-submarine battle. The most important was the AS (Air Search) series of radar sets which could be carried in TBFs and TBMs. The first radar tested in Avengers was the AS model B which was installed in some TBFs during late 1942. It was followed by ASD the next year, which had to be fitted in a bulbous fairing on the leading edge of one wing.

But the most valuable airborne radar was the British-developed ASV which operated on a 10cm wavelength. Its greatest asset was its relatively light weight — always an important consideration in the overloaded Avenger series. ASV possessed greater accuracy and definition than most other airborne radars, and was also less liable to be successfully jammed. All the AS sets were used primarily against surface targets, though air-to-air scanning was possible within a limited range.

Another important anti-submarine aid was the sonobuoy, available in June 1943. This was an expendable listening device which could be dropped from an Avenger to help track down a submarine. It consisted of a hydrophone for detecting underwater noises and a radio transmitter which relayed

Right: Loading Mark 10, Mod 5 mines in a TBF-1 aboard USS *Lexington* on 29 March 1944. This action against the Palau Islands was the only occasion when US carrier aircraft employed mines during World War II. / *National Archives*

Below: Sonobuoys, an important anti-submarine weapon, in the bomb bay of a *Bogue* Avenger. / *National Archives*

the sounds to the aircraft. It was a prominent feature in the destruction of numerous Axis submarines.

Some Avengers were fitted with spotlights to provide continuous illumination of nocturnal targets. This was yet another anti-submarine feature, but was met with mixed emotions by most aircrews. While it fully lit up a U-Boat during the run-in to attack, it also provided an excellent aiming point for the sub's AA gunners. Natural moonlight or long-burning flares were more preferred methods of illumination.

Finally, near the end of the war, the Avenger's turret-mounted .50cal was given a serious rethinking. The turret and the gun itself, if removed, enabled a considerable weight saving, and thought was given to installing a swivel-mounted twin .30cal set in its place. Some night-flying squadrons discarded their turrets in the Pacific, but otherwise the suggestion was not adopted. This was largely due to the objections of Commander Fleet Air Atlantic, who wanted the .50s superior firepower to suppress flak from U-Boats operating on a fight-back basis. But at the end of 1944 the tunnel-mounted .30cal for the radioman was removed from many squadron aircraft and was eliminated on Eastern's production line altogether.

The Avenger's defensive armament served it well during the period 1942-44 in the Pacific. But from autumn 1944, with fewer bombers on fast carriers due to greatly enlarged fighter squadrons, very few Japanese aircraft got through to attack any TBMs. In fact, from 1943 to 1945 the Hellcats and Corsairs provided such efficient protection that only 20 Avengers were known lost to Japanese planes, and only five of these fell in the last eight months of the war.

Sub Killer

The Atlantic Gap was a dreadful fact of life for Allied merchant ships during most of World War II. Despite long-range patrol aircraft based in Newfoundland, in Iceland and the British Isles, there still existed a 500-1200 mile stretch along the North Atlantic convoy routes beyond air cover. Not even British acquisition of bases in the Azores in late 1943 significantly closed what merchant sailors called the black pit. In this area, German U-Boats preyed off Allied convoys without fear of air attack.

Until the spring of 1943.

At the end of 1941 the US Maritime Commission released 20 freighter hulls for conversion to escort aircraft carriers, designated CVEs. Ten went to the US Navy and 10 to Britain. They were followed by four converted tankers and then by the 50-ship Casablanca class, all built from the keel up as carriers. But CVEs were all approximately similar: an overall length of 500-550ft, top speed of 17-19kts and capable of operating up to 30 aircraft.

By early March 1943 the first American submarine hunter-killer unit was operational. This was the *Bogue* group, composed of four World War I destroyers grouped around the first American CVE employed in convoy escort. *Bogue* operated Composite Squadron 9 (VC-9) under Lt-Cdr William M. Drane, and initially flew a dozen F4F-4 Wildcats and eight TBF-1s. The Avenger was immediately recognised as a natural for this sort of work. Its range, endurance and carrying capacity suited it ideally to both the search and strike roles required for hunting German submarines.

There were plenty to hunt. In March there were an average of 116 U-Boats at sea each day; one-third on station, two-thirds in transit to base or operating area. That month they sank 108 merchant ships for over 620,000 gross tons. The Battle of the Atlantic was still in doubt.

Bogue escorted three convoys during March and April, with a rather inauspicious beginning. Heavy seas and poor flying weather cancelled many search missions. Only two U-Boats were seen, and neither was attacked.

But the aerial hunter-killers were learning.

Early experience demonstrated that submarines did in fact have to be actively hunted. Simply maintaining an 'umbrella' over a convoy was small deterrent to a determined U-Boat skipper, who could slip in and fire his torpedoes before being spotted. Avenger search patterns were expanded to fan out ahead and on both flanks of the convoy, thereby increasing probability of an early contact. The complement was altered to include only nine Wildcats and increased to 12 Avengers, as the TBFs were more versatile. And search teams were composed generally of one F4F and a TBF for flexibility and mutual support.

The new techniques brought results. In the late evening of 21 May *Bogue* was escorting the westbound convoy ON-184 when the VC-9 squadron commander, Lt-Cdr Drane, spotted a surfaced U-Boat 60 miles ahead of the convoy. Drane pushed his Avenger into a dive on U-231 and made an accurate bombing attack which badly damaged the sub's bridge. The U-Boat was not sunk, but its damage was such that it headed east for repair in port.

Next day business picked up dramatically. Early that morning a TBF found a U-Boat surfacing 55 miles from *Bogue*. The pilot took advantage of low-lying clouds to conceal his approach, but was seen by the sub's lookouts and forced to abandon his attack due to heavy AA fire. Communications problems prevented reinforcement aircraft from arriving in time for a co-ordinated attack.

At the same time, another TBF sighted a second sub 35 miles ahead of the convoy and descended to strike, but was foiled when the U-Boat 'pulled the plug' and dived while still out of range.

During mid-morning a third U-Boat was caught napping by Ensign Stewart E. Doty in a TBF, who ruptured the pressure hull with a near-miss by one of four bombs he dropped. This boat, U-305, dived to make temporary repairs and surfaced about three hours later only to be pounced upon by another Avenger. Like the first sub, this one considered itself fortunate and shaped course for Brest.

'Third time Lucky' had not held true on

War is hell — but isn't always hot. The U-boat campaign went on full time, as these escort carrier sailors learned while clearing a snowbound flight deck in the North Atlantic during the winter of 1942-43. / *Grumman*

23 May, but the fourth contact of the day held the charm. A radio direction finder bearing in the afternoon had put U-569 only 20 miles from *Bogue* just as an Avenger piloted by Lt(jg) William F. Chamberlain spotted it. Chamberlain quickly attacked and dropped all four bombs close aboard the sub, which crash-dived. The hunters of VC-9 knew they had not sunk the boat, and literally kept on top of it through the rest of the afternoon. When U-569 surfaced, Lt Howard S. Roberts was right there. He dropped a full spread of four depth charges which did not prevent the sub from diving, but she had to come up again almost immediately, and scuttled.

Thus, U-569 was the first kill made by the US Navy's aerial hunter-killer teams. The first Axis submarine sunk by Avengers had been a Vichy French boat sent to the bottom

Top: This excellent photo may have been taken aboard USS *Bogue* in 1944. The Avenger's exhaust stack has been modified with a flame dampener for added security during night operations, as the hunt for U-boats by then was a round-the-clock business. / *Grumman*

Above: Avengers and Wildcats on anti-submarine duty aboard USS *Card* in 1943. Note that the wartime censor has blanked out the radar antenna immediately below the F4F's wing. From August to November 1943, *Card* aircraft sank eight U-Boats. / *Grumman*

Above: First blood. Lt Howard Roberts of VC-9 off USS *Bogue* dropped four Mk 17 Mod II depth bombs from his TBF-1 in this attack on U-569, 22 May 1943. The submarine was sunk as a result; the first success by a US Navy 'hunter-killer' carrier aircraft. Two bombs are visible in the photo. / *National Archives*

strike. The trend continued into the second quarter of 1943, as merchant losses were cut to 150 ships of less than a million tons while U-Boat losses for those three months almost doubled to 73. For the first time the kill-loss ratio of ships to submarines plunged to near parity, at only two to one. It had not previously been below six to one.

From the escort carriers' viewpoint, July 1943 was the definite turnaround in the U-Boat campaign. *Core* with VC-13 embarked and *Santee* with VC-29 made their first kills that month which, combined with *Bogue*, accounted for six sinkings. But it was not all one-sided.

When Admiral Karl Dönitz, the U-Boat commander, learned that carrier aircraft were operating in the North Atlantic, he took quick action. In April he ordered heavier anti-aircraft armament installed on his boats, and instructed his skippers to stand and fight any aircraft. It took time for these orders to be implemented, but in mid-July the Avenger crews began discovering for themselves how formidable the AA defences could be. With four 20mm guns and a 37mm, a U-Boat could put up a terrific amount of flak.

On the afternoon of 13 July a VC-13 team off *Core* caught the 1,600 ton tanker U-487 on the surface. The Wildcat dived to strafe and suppress AA fire but was solidly hit by the automatic weapons and crashed into the ocean. Three more aircraft were summoned to the scene and made a co-ordinated attack which split the defences. An Avenger bored in close enough to drop all four bombs, and U-487 was finished.

Till now, all Avenger sub kills had been made by bombs or depth charges. But the next day, 14 July, a new weapon was employed. A VC-29 team off *Santee* sighted U-160 on the surface that morning, and the Wildcat went down to strafe according to new doctrine. The attack induced the sub to dive, which was just what the TBF pilot was waiting for. Lt (jg) John Ballentine dropped his Fido torpedo which homed in on the boat's engines and scored a direct hit. An underwater explosion erupted to the surface, and U-160 never came back up. Less than 24 hours later another *Santee* Avenger scored a kill with a Fido. Then on the 16th a VC-13 TBF from *Core* killed U-67 with a load of bombs. The CVEs had sent four U-Boats to the bottom in four consecutive days. *Bogue* and *Santee* Avengers made the last two kills of the month using depth charges and a Fido.

Six more kills came in August, including four by VC-1 aboard *Card*. No sub sinkings were made by CVE planes in September. But during October, *Card*, *Core* and *Croatan* aircraft executed 20 attacks, claiming 12 kills. In truth 'only' six of these claims were

off Casablanca by three Scouting Squadron 27 TBFs from *Suwannee* during the North African invasion in November 1942. But that was an isolated incident unrelated to the Battle of the Atlantic. *Bogue's* convoy ON-184 completed its passage without loss of a single ship, which was in itself remarkable. Some convoys were losing 40% of their merchantmen at this time.

Bogue aircraft sank two more U-Boats in June, but the mere tally of sinkings was only a small part of the shifting trend towards eventual victory in the Atlantic. In the last three months of 1942, U-Boats sank over 300 merchant ships for nearly 1,800,000 gross tons. In the first quarter of 1943, the period when CVE aircraft began covering the Atlantic Gap, merchant sinkings dropped to 243. Patrolling Avengers and Wildcats had discouraged many large-scale wolfpack attacks on escorted convoys by sighting the U-Boats before they were positioned to

accurate, but undoubtedly other U-Boats were damaged. The hunter-killer TBFs and F4Fs thought five submarines were destroyed during November, but *Bogue* with VC-19 now embarked finished the year with single kills in the last two months of 1943.

American escort carriers sank 23 U-Boats from May through December, nearly all by Avengers. Working with destroyers and other anti-submarine vessels, they trimmed shipping losses in the last quarter of 1943 to 89 ships of less than half a million tons. A year before it was not unusual to lose that much in a single month. The most successful squadron was VC-9, with eight kills during 1943. Half had been scored while flying from *Bogue* under Lt-Cdr Drane, and half from *Card* under Lt-Cdr H. M. Avery. Then the squadron served aboard *Solomons* for two months in 1944, still led by Avery, and got a ninth U-Boat. But it was no pushover.

On 15 June 1944 an RDF fix indicated a

Above: A TBF flies low over a carrier deck crowded with Avengers and Wildcats. The US Navy's Atlantic Theatre colour scheme is shown: insignia white overall with gull grey sides and upper surfaces. Barely visible under the airborne TBF's starboard wing is the 1944 style national insignia. / *Grumman*

Left: This remarkable photo shows the first rocket attack against a U-Boat. A VC-58 Avenger caught the submarine on the surface, and the trail of two HVARs is clearly visible. / *National Archives*

submarine nearby, and Ensign George E. Edwards sniffed it out. The U-Boats still believed in the fight-back policy, and U-860 shot down Edwards' Avenger before he could get off a position report. A thorough search pattern turned up the troublesome boat again at dusk when the CO himself, Lt-Cdr Avery, found U-860 on the surface. The squadron leader knew he stood little chance of sinking the sub unassisted, but astutely judged that it would stand and fight. He kept it occupied with strafing runs for 20min while homing in three other aircraft. Despite the increased odds, U-860 remained surfaced to shoot it out as darkness fell. Lt(jg) Chamberlain, who had damaged U-569 in the squadron's first kill over a year before, pressed his attack to point-blank range. His bombs exploded just as he passed overhead, destroying both victor and victim in the blast.

Three months earlier a similar incident had occurred. On 19 March a VC-6 team off *Block Island* found the 'milch cow' U-1059 early in the morning. Some of the Germans were enjoying a swim when the Wildcat dived to strafe the sub, but her AA guns were manned immediately and the Avenger was hit during its attack. The TBM pilot, Lt(Jg) Norman Dowty, ignored the damage and continued his run. He released two depth bombs, one of which exploded in the sub's ammunition locker, and both Avenger and U-Boat were destroyed. One of Dowty's crew was rescued along with seven Germans.

That was the only U-Boat sunk by *Block Island* aircraft, though the destroyers of her screen sent five subs to the bottom. Admiral

Above: **This VC-58 crew off USS *Block Island* was credited with making the first US Navy rocket attack against an enemy submarine. The pilot, Lt(jg) Leonard L. McFord (centre), sighted the U-Boat. His crewmen were ARM3/c Charles Gertsch and AMM2/c William H. Ryder. A kill was claimed, but postwar records failed to confirm loss of a U-Boat on the date in question, 11 January 1944.** / *Grumman*

Right: **Submarines were sometimes the lesser enemy, as demonstrated by the rolling deck of this escort carrier running through heavy Atlantic swells.** / *Grumman*

Dönitz exacted revenge on 29 March when a U-Boat put a spread of torpedoes into the CVE, but she was the only US carrier sunk in the entire campaign.

In all, US Navy escort carrier planes sank nine submarines in the Atlantic during 1944. The last of these was on 20 August when several VC-69 TBMs off *Bogue* sank U-1229. Thus, *Bogue's* aircraft had put under the first and last U-Boat sunk by American hunter-killer aircraft. But though 1944 sinkings were considerably fewer than the year before, things were even rougher for the submarines. Previously they had been free from air attack at night, and a nocturnal surface engagement was a favourite U-Boat technique. But no more.

The first CVE night operations were inaugurated by *Card* in February 1944. Two TBFs had been specially modified to fill the 'Night Owl' role. They were stripped of all unessential equipment and personnel. Guns, ordnance and armour plate were all removed to allow installation of extra fuel tanks which, if necessary, could give each Avenger a 14-hour endurance. The pilot was accompanied only by a radar operator. At dusk on 13 February the two Avengers were launched, and patrolled 80 miles to either side of the convoy. Without weaons they had no means to attack a submarine, but they were intended solely to direct destroyers to the contact. Though no U-Boats were found during this brief experiment, it led the way to less impromptu measures.

Composite Squadron 58 under Cdr Richard Gould went aboard *Guadalcanal* at Norfolk, Virginia during March. The captain was Daniel V. Gallery, a colourful, popular officer who believed CVEs could fly their planes round the clock. Both Gould and the Landing Signal Officer agreed to try Gallery's idea for full-time night flying, and the squadron was trained accordingly.

The plan was to keep four armed Avengers in the air during the night. Since they were not modified to carry extra fuel, they were comfortably limited to four hours on each patrol and would therefore require relief. This meant *Guadalcanal* would operate eight Avengers in two relays each night. After the pilots had qualified for night CVE landings, rough weather was the only factor which posed a serious threat to the plan.

Composite Squadron 58 began its night patrols on 7 April, hunting south of the Azores. The first night brought no contacts, but the night of the eighth an Avenger surprised U-515 charging her batteries on the surface. The TBM delivered a depth bomb attack which forced the boat down only 30 miles from the carrier. Other Avengers were delegated to remain on the scene while three destroyers sped to the contact point.

Twice during the night the U-Boat came up, but was forced under as soon as it broke surface. All next morning and into the afternoon the destroyers tracked the submarine, delivering depth charge attacks. Heavily damaged, U-515 surfaced within gun range of the escorts, but merely to allow her crew to abandon ship.

The VC-58 Avengers did not have to share the next kill. A hundred miles to the southeast another sub was tracked down by the night flying TBMs and was caught at dawn, running east. Two Avengers and a Wildcat came out of the darkness to the west, their target silhouetted against the sunrise. U-68 attempted to crash-dive but it was too late. She was literally blown in two by a combination of depth bombs and rockets.

As 'Cap'n Dan' Gallery related: 'This settled all doubt about night operations. In a month of constant daylight flying, we had seen no subs. In 48 hours of night operations, we had two kills.'

The 30 U-Boats sunk by US CVE aircraft and two shared kills with destroyers during 1943-44 were a very small portion of the total 780 sent to the bottom during the entire war. But the Battle of the Atlantic had so dramatically reversed course by the last year of the war that no sinkings were made by Avengers or Wildcats in the five months before VE-Day. The day-to-day impact of the escort carrier squadrons, their mere presence, was almost beyond computation. How many submarine attacks were spoiled or prevented can never be fully known.

In the Pacific, however, 1945 was by far

Below: Sometimes a capture is worth more than a kill. This was certainly the case on 4 June 1944 when the hunter-killer team based around the escort carrier *Guadalcanal* forced U-505 to the surface and boarded her. A TBF flies low over the abandoned submarine, at this point in danger of sinking. But the boarding party closed her seacocks and prevented a successful scuttling. / *Grumman*

Left: Admiral Reed and Captain Vosseler pose with the trophies of the hunt: USS *Bogue's* scoreboard showing 12 Axis submarines claimed sunk by *Bogue* aircraft as of October 1944. / *National Archives*

Below: An Avenger on anti-sub patrol over the Fast Carrier Task Force in the Pacific. US Navy battleships, destroyers, and carriers are clearly visible behind the TBF — prime targets for Japanese submarines. But after 1942 no American flattops were lost to the undersea menace. On the other hand, Avengers sank six Japanese fleet submarines from 1943-45 and shared in the destruction of two more. The number of midget subs destroyed has not been tallied. / *Grumman*

the most active year for Avenger sub hunters. The only previous period of much activity had occurred during November 1943 and the invasion of the Gilbert Islands. *Chenango* planes sank I-21 on the 29th. But as in the Atlantic, an enemy sub picked off a CVE, and *Liscome Bay* went down in 23 minutes after being hit by torpedoes from I-175 on 24 November.

Only two sub kills were made by Avengers in the Pacific during 1944. The first occurred on 19 June, at the height of the Battle of the Philippine Sea, when Ensign G. E. Sabin of Torpedo Squadron 60 off *Suwannee* sent I-184 into a final dive near Guam in the Marianas. Five months later, on 18 November, *Anzio* aircraft teamed with a destroyer escort to end the career of I-41 some 300 miles east of Samar.

Anzio was to the Pacific CVEs what *Bogue* was to those in the Atlantic: the first and last hunter-killer to sink an enemy sub, and the most successful to boot. During the bloody battle for Iwo Jima, *Anzio's* VC-13 sank two submarines on consecutive days: an RO boat of 960 tons on 26 February and a big I-boat on the 27th.

Composite Squadron 92 off *Tulagi* finished an I-boat at the end of April, during the Okinawa campaign, and then *Anzio* scored again a month later, sinking I-361 unassisted. *Anzio's* last victim was unlucky I-13, destroyed in collaboration with a destroyer escort on 16 July, some 550 miles east of Yokosuka. Of the six sub kills credited to CVEs in the Pacific, *Anzio* accounted for three by herself plus both of the shared kills. The sinking of Japanese midget subs is difficult, perhaps impossible, to document.

To round out the story, however, we must return to the Atlantic in June 1944, only five days after *Suwannee* aircraft put I-184 on the bottom off Guam. The I-52 was on a special liaison mission to France and was first located by a night-flying Avenger off *Bogue*, south-west of the Azores on 23 June. Lt-Cdr Jesse Taylor, VC-69's CO, subsequently picked up the radar contact and dropped a flare which illuminated the 350ft monster, drove it down with a bombing attack, and dropped a sonobuoy. Though the Japanese skipper evaded Taylor, he survived only a few hours. Shortly before 0100 on the 24th another *Bogue* Avenger followed sonobuoy contacts and executed a depth-bomb attack in the midnight darkness. After dawn a destroyer patrolling the area picked up a Japanese sandal and five dozen bales of crude rubber floating among the assorted debris.

The final tally of submarine sinkings for US Navy CVE aircraft was 31 in the Atlantic (including one Japanese and one Vichy French) and six in the Pacific, plus two German and two Japanese boats shared with

Top: A depth bomb explodes close aboard a surfaced U-Boat, 'somewhere in the Atlantic'. Two crewmen are clearly visible at the base of the anti-aircraft mount.

Right: What to claim? A TBF circles low over the spot where it has depth-charged a submarine contact. Often accurate assessment of such attacks was impossible until captured enemy records were available for reference after the war.

escort vessels. The campaign which the Avenger waged in the Atlantic was probably as typical of war itself as any aspect of World War II. Mostly it was hours and days and weeks of dull routine; of monotonous, uneventful patrols during which nothing was seen and almost nothing happened.

Then there were the few times when a contact actually developed into an attack. And then there was too much to do in the time available. The sub had to be reported with an accurate position fix, and additional aircraft summoned. The attack had to be co-ordinated and delivered, often in the face of formidable AA fire. There was the constant gnawing anxiety that this opportunity — the one thing for which the pilot and crew had trained for months and might never come again — could somehow go wrong. And sometimes it did. The aim was hurried or misjudged. The sub dived while still out of range. Or the attacking aircraft fell to well-directed automatic weapons fire.

But now and then, just often enough to keep up morale, a tangible result was

obtained in the form of a definite kill. Oil slick and debris bubbling to the surface, the sight of U-Boat men bobbing in the water, or even the spectacle of a sub breaking in two and plunging out of sight. These were the sensational, dramatic consequences of a successful attack.

However, they were not the most important result. They were not the end, but the means to an end. The undramatic, unheralded but war-winning result was a merchant convoy arriving intact at its destination, with few or no losses.

It would be unfair and inaccurate to say the Avenger was largely responsible for winning the Battle of the Atlantic. But there can be no doubt that it was the dominant aircraft enaged in that six-year struggle — the only aspect of the war which Winston Churchill feared the Allies might lose. Because of the crucial importance of keeping open the sea lanes between the Old World and the New, the Avenger's part in defeating the U-Boats must be considered its most significant contribution to victory.

Fleet Air Arm

The British Royal Navy received its first 15 TBF-1s before the end of 1942. Suffering an acute shortage of modern carrier-based strike aircraft, the Fleet Air Arm quickly took to the Avenger. But until early 1944 the TBF was known as the Tarpon in British service — after the large warm water fish of the western Atlantic.

Britain received nearly a thousand TBFs and TBMs: 402 TBF-1s as Avenger Is, 334 TBM-1s as Mark IIs, and 222 TBM-3s as Mark IIIs. Fourteen FAA squadrons flew Avengers during the war, all but one being carrier-based. Additionally, one Royal New Zealand Air Force squadron flew TBFs in the South Pacific.

Whether Tarpon or Avenger, the big Grumman was badly needed by the Commonwealth services. The ageing but tireless Fairey Swordfish remained in service until the end of the war, but the 'Stringbags' biplane design, with limited speed and range, clearly marked it as obsolete. Of questionable value was Fairey's follow-on, the ungainly looking Barracuda torpedo plane-dive bomber. The Barracuda suffered a six-year gestation period, and by the time it became available in any numbers, it was past its prime. Recalled one veteran FAA pilot: 'The Barracuda was a good dive bomber. Everytime you reduced power it went into a dive.' By October 1944 Avenger had replaced the Barracudas aboard the British Pacific Fleet carriers.

Yet another Fairey strike aircraft, the versatile Firefly, arrived late in the war. It was a modern, useful machine; heavily armed with good range. However, as a two-seater it was neither a fighter nor a bomber. It was, perhaps, the first purely naval strike aircraft. So the Avenger was the FAA's main carrier-based bomber for most of two years.

The first FAA Avenger squadron was No 832, formed at Norfolk, Virginia, in late 1942. This coincided with the refit of HMS *Victorious* at Norfolk Navy Yard during December and January. By that spring, *Victorious* was in the South Pacific training with USS *Saratoga*. The 15 Tarpons of No 832 Squadron flew from *Victorious* with

Below: **The number six man joins formation in a starboard echelon.** / *IWM*

Bottom: **A Fleet Air Arm Avenger taxying with folded wings. This design was similar to that of the wing-fold mechanism of the F4F Wildcat, which Leroy R. Grumman designed using a bent paper clip and a rubber eraser as a model.** / *IWM*

Top right: Pilots and aircrew of the Fleet Air Arm in training with TBF-1s at the US Naval Air Station at Squantum, Massachussets. Of interest is the mixture of American and British equipment, life vests, parachute harnesses, and flying helmets. / *Grumman*

Centre right: Watch that first step! Climbing on the wing of Avenger I FN795 was not easy as this officer discovered. Note the bulged fuselage window, peculiar to British Avengers for improved visibility. / *IWM*

Right: A Tarpon I takes off from Roosevelt Field on Long Island during acceptance tests. / *IWM*

Below: TBF-1s (Tarpon Mark Is) on the ramp with F6F-3 Hellcats at the Grumman factory in 1943. / *Grumman*

three FAA Martlet fighter squadrons on missions over the Solomon Islands in June and July 1943. The objective was to prevent the Japanese Navy from interfering with the invasion of the New Georgia group, but as the enemy fleet failed to contest the landings, little happened. *Victorious* returned to Britain, leaving some of her TBFs with *Saratoga.*

Like their US Navy counterparts, FAA Avengers hunted U-Boats. But they were engaged on a far smaller scale, as the venerable Swordfish was much more numerous aboard British CVEs in European waters. From 1940 to 1945, FAA aircraft sank 18 Axis submarines and shared in 16 other sinkings with escort vessels or RAF units. The biplane Swordfish accounted for 15 of the solo kills and participated in another 10.

But the Avenger was the next most-successful FAA sub-hunter. Four U-boats succumbed in whole or part to Royal Navy TBMs. No 846 Squadron was the premier Avenger unit when it came to tracking down submarines, being credited with one whole kill and two assists.

The squadron's first two successes came within three days of one another in early April 1944. Escorting Arctic convoy RA-58, No 846 Squadron was embarked aboard HMS *Tracker* while Swordfish of No 819 Squadron flew from *Activity.* The two units hunted aggressively, and on the first of the month No 846 Squadron Avengers helped HMS *Beagle* sniff out and run to bay U-355. Two days later No 819's Swordfish joined *Tracker* Avengers in finishing off U-288.

The Avenger's only sub kill in the Indian Ocean was very much a team effort. TBMs from No 832 Squadron aboard HMS *Begum* and No 851 Squadron on *Shah* destroyed U-198 on 12 August 1944 in concert with a British and an Indian frigate.

There were no more anti-sub successes for FAA Avengers until the last month of the European war. On 4 May 1945 three Royal Navy CVEs launched 44 Avengers and Wildcats against German shipping at Kilbotn, Norway. No 846 Squadron, now

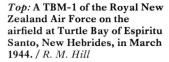

Top: A TBM-1 of the Royal New Zealand Air Force on the airfield at Turtle Bay of Espiritu Santo, New Hebrides, in March 1944. / *R. M. Hill*

Above: Avenger Is warming up their engines on the flight line of a naval air station. / *Grumman*

73

Left: FAA Avengers conducted numerous strikes in Scandanavian waters against German warships and other Axis shipping targets. This photo was taken during the approach to Svino Fjord on the rocky Norwegian coast. / *IWM*

Below: That big wing provided lots of lift, as proven by the catapulting of a No 845 Squadron Avenger I from HMS *Ameer* in Trincomalee Harbour, Ceylon. / *IWM*

embarked in HMS *Trumpeter*, did most of the damage. Her Avengers sank a moored depot ship and U-711 which was secured alongside. HMS *Queen's* No 853 Squadron sank another ship in the same attack, the last FAA conducted in Europe. One bomber and one fighter were lost to anti-aircraft fire. Three days later, Germany surrendered.

Undoubtedly the most successful operation in which the Avenger participated with the Royal Navy was the two-part strike on Sumatran oil fields in January 1945. This was Operation Meridian, involving four carriers: *Indomitable* with No 857 Squadron; *Illustrious* with No 854; *Victorious* with No 849; and *Indefatigable* embarking No 820. These squadrons totalled 65 Avengers, supported by some 170 Hellcats, Corsairs, Seafires and Fireflies.

The first strike was launched against facilities at Pladjoe, with 47 Avengers all armed with four 500lb bombs. Another flight of four attacked known Japanese airfields in the area. Hellcats and Corsairs provided escort.

Things did not go well with the TBMs in the beginning. Seven Avengers were forced to abort or were damaged in flight deck accidents. But surprise was achieved. No fighter interception was made until after the target had been hit, and not even the flak began until the TBMs were in their dives. The bombing was accurate, with considerable damage inflicted upon the refinery.

There was surprise for the aircrews, too. During their dive to bombing height they were astonished to see barrage balloons suddenly in their midst. No aircraft struck these obstacles, but they boded no good for the future. Two Avengers, one from *Indomitable* and one from *Indefatigable*,

failed to return. The former was shot down by a Japanese fighter.

In all, the carriers had lost nine aircraft but Pladjoe's facilities were estimated 30% destroyed. Five days later the task force returned to Sumatran waters, on 29 January, to deal with Soengi Gerong. The strike group composition was nearly identical to that of the 24th. The bomber leader was Lt-Cdr W. J. Mainprice, CO of *Illustrious'* No 854 Squadron. He was informed that any balloons protecting the next target would be destroyed before his formation arrived.

The strike was launched early in the morning under low ceiling and reduced visibility. One Avenger lost power and splashed down into a water landing while

Bottom left, top and above:
'Goodbye, welcome back and try again.' The three phases of flying off aircraft carriers are illustrated in these three photos. A *Trumpeter* Avenger I is catapulted off and another snags the number one wire of *Ravager*. In the third photo, An Avenger III takes a 'wave around' after overshooting the mark and will make another circuit. The British Pacific Fleet adopted US style horizontal bars to the blue and white cockade as further insurance against confusing friendly with enemy aircraft insignia. / *IWM*

An Avenger after it had
successfully landed in the sea
when its engine failed on
leaving the carrier. The crew
were rescued a few minutes
after the picture was taken.
/ IWM

Below: Dawn launch from HMS *Illustrious* 'somewhere at sea'. This aircraft is from either No 845 or No 854 Squadron. */IWM*

Bottom: Gear coming up, an Avenger climbs on take-off. The pilot's control input is visible in the amount of right rudder necessary to offset the Wright R-2600's propeller rotation. Rudder trim alone would not always compensate. */IWM*

three more returned to their ships with engine trouble.

This time there was no surprise. Japanese fighters were up and waiting, the AA guns were alerted, and most of the balloons were still aloft. Despite this formidable defence, the TBMs pressed their attacks with determination and accuracy. But Lt-Cdr Mainprice, the strike leader, hit a balloon cable during his dive towards the target and was killed with his crew. His wingman's plane was also snagged by a cable, with loss of all aboard.

Departing the burning oil tanks and bombed facilities, the Avengers headed for rendezvous in singles and small formations. At this point they were vulnerable to interception and No 849 Squadron lost two aircraft to defending fighters. But the Avengers could defend themselves, too. A pair of No 820 Squadron pilots off *Indefatigable* fought a Tojo which expended its ammunition in numerous passes, then pulled up in front of Sub-Lt W. Coster. Coster fired all his .50cal load at the fighter, which was last seen dropping towards the trees, streaming smoke and flame.

78

Lt G. J. Connolly of No 854 Squadron spotted two Tojos harrying a No 849 Squadron Avenger low over the treetops. Diving to the attack, he shot down one Japanese and, drawing the attention of the other, was able to disengage and escort the damaged *Victorious* bomber to the task force. Numerous Avengers were shot up from flak and fighters — the crews complained about lack of adequate protection — and six ditched near the fleet. Fortunately these crews were rescued, but 19 pilots or aircrew were lost with 11 Avengers shot down or force-landed.

However, the Grummans were mainly responsible for cutting Sumatra's aviation fuel production by two-thirds at a time when Japan could least afford it. The British Pacific Fleet TBMs continued their work at Okinawa, Formosa and over Japan itself for the remainder of the year. Thus the Avenger was a success in two navies in both hemispheres. Few aircraft can claim a similar record.

Top: **Tarpon torpedo bombers in beam formation during exercises.** / *IWM*

Above: **23 May 1945. Avengers from carriers of the British Pacific Fleet flying over Sakishima Gunto on the way to bomb military installations during the continuing attacks.** / *IWM*

Wrecks and Battle Damage

Left: Apparently the victim of a forced landing, this early production TBF-1 nosed up in a rough field, probably on Long Island in 1942. / *Grumman*

Top: A VT-11 Avenger showing battle damage upon return to Guadalcanal in the summer of 1943. / *O'Malley*

Above: One that got away. Lt R. R. 'Railroad' Jones of VT-10 was fortunate to bring his Avenger back to *Enterprise* following the epic raid on Truk Atoll on 16 February 1944. Clearly visible are bullet holes in the leading edge of the port wing, testifying to the marksmanship of a Zero pilot who attacked Jones. The enemy fighter was driven off by another Torpedo 10 pilot. / *Jones*

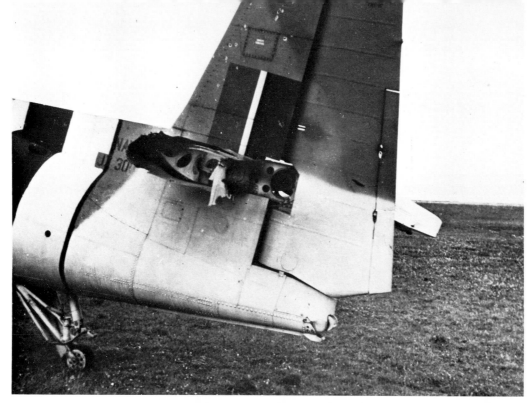

This page: Avenger JZ-300 was badly shot up during a glide-bombing attack on German shipping at St Malo, France, on the Brittany Coast. Sub-Lt Thomas Derrick-White, probably of No 855 Squadron, was one of six Fleet Air Arm pilots on the strike. His JZ-300 was hit by light and medium flak during the low-level pullout, and he ordered his crew to stand by for a water landing. Himself wounded in the back, Derrick-White did not know that the observer riding behind him was dead. But once out to sea, the Avenger proved controllable and was brought to a fast landing in miserable weather at a British coastal airfield. Only when the surviving crew members climbed out did they realise how fortunate they had been. The port stabiliser and elevator were gone, a five-inch hole was in the other stabiliser, and the canopy was shattered by 36 holes. Derrick-White concluded that Avengers were 'the planes to put your trust in'. / Grumman

Left: Plucked Turkey. This battle-scarred TBF-1C was abandoned in a South Pacific 'boneyard', where it was photographed in January 1944. It has been cannibalised for all possible spare parts. Wing panels and tail surfaces have been taken off, instruments and armament removed. / *Grumman*

Below: Ensign T. B. Long of VT-2 wrote off this TBF in a crash landing aboard USS *Hornet* in June of 1944. / *National Archives*

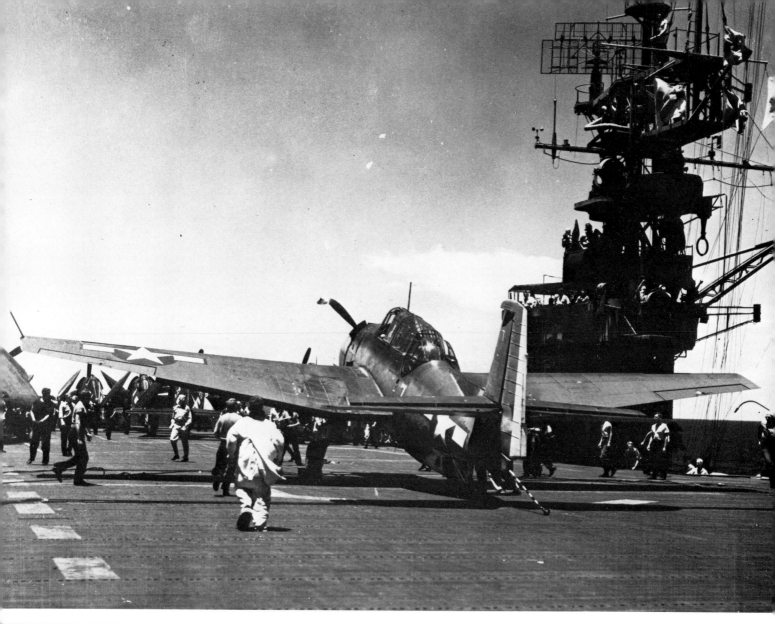

Above: Firefighters and deck hands rush to the aid of this VT-31 TBM, which has just experienced a rough landing aboard the light carrier *Cabot* on 11 July 1944.

Left: A broken arresting wire allowed this TBF, unlucky 13, to crash into the island of USS *Bogue*, operating in the Atlantic during July 1944.
/ National Archives

Above right: Composite Squadron 21 aboard the escort carrier *Marcus Island* lost this TBM-1C overboard in August 1944. The Avenger sheared off its starboard wing, taking a floater raft with it (visible under the right wingroot). The pilot is unharmed, and is removing his parachute harness. */ R. M. Hill*

Right: This VT-15 pilot brought his Avenger back to USS *Essex* with a dead turret gunner during operations in the Philippines during November 1944. */ National Archives*

A mobile crane attempts to retrieve a TBM which nearly went over the bow of the escort carrier *Charger* during operations in January 1945. / *Grumman*

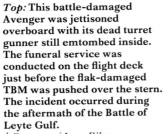

Top: This battle-damaged Avenger was jettisoned overboard with its dead turret gunner still emtombed inside. The funeral service was conducted on the flight deck just before the flak-damaged TBM was pushed over the stern. The incident occurred during the aftermath of the Battle of Leyte Gulf. / *Grumman/Acme Films*

Above: Large-calibre anti-aircraft shells punched huge holes in both wings of this VT-84 TBM-3, which still managed to return to *Bunker Hill* on 19 March 1945. The two crewmen are climbing out while a plane captain assists the pilot. / *R. M. Hill*

Right: A VT-83 TBM from USS *Essex* heads toward a water landing, its tail shredded by AA fire during the Okinawa campaign in April 1945. / *National Archives*

Above: TBM-3 from VT-82, USS *Bennington,* 1945. The pilot made a safe water landing. / *Liberator Club collection*

Right: This TBM nosed up on landing aboard the escort carrier *Rudyerd Bay* barely missing other Avengers parked forward. / *J. F. Curtis*

The Way West

Above: A TBF makes a run on a burning Japanese cargo ship during the 4 December 1943 raid on Kwajalein Atoll in the Marshalls. / *Grumman*

Left: The meaning of air support. US Marines watch a flight of five TBFs attacking Japanese positions on the north end of Namur Island, Kwajalein Atoll, in early February 1944. Scenes like this were repeated across the Central Pacific as Avengers provided tactical air cover for ground troops. / *Grumman*

Left: An Essex class carrier with a full deckload of aircraft, vintage 1943. In addition to TBFs are F6F Hellcats and SB2C Helldivers, the standard complement for fleet carriers during the last two years of the war. A Fletcher class destroyer trails the carrier. / *Grumman*

Below: A low-flying TBF banks for another run against a manoeuvring Japanese destroyer in Truk Lagoon, 16 February 1944. / *Grumman*

Right: Torpedo wakes criss-cross Truk Lagoon during the big attack by US carriers on 16-17 February 1944. The freighter in the foreground has just been struck forward of amidships while another 'fish' seems headed for a hit. Some 200,000 tons of naval and merchant shipping was sunk at Truk, in large part by TBFs. / *Grumman*

Below right: An Asashio class destroyer is obscured in smoke and spray as an Avenger passes low overhead during the first Truk raid. This ship, though apparently at anchor, was not sunk. But four other Japanese destroyers were lost during the two-day strike in mid-February 1944. / *Grumman*

Left: Wounded turret gunner Kenneth Bratton is removed from his TBF aboard USS *Saratoga* following a carrier strike against Japanese warships at Rabaul Harbour, New Britain in November 1943.

Below: Leading the way west were the new-generation fast carriers. This is USS *Yorktown* (CV-10), second ship of the 27,000 ton Essex class. She was named for CV-5, which was sunk in the Battle of Midway during June 1942. The second *Yorktown* was in combat almost continuously from autumn 1943 until the end of the war.

Bottom left: The kamikazes first appeared in the Philippines campaign. Here a twin-engine suicider narrowly misses an escort carrier, photographed from a sister ship in the same task group with two Avengers tied down on the flight deck.

Above: But this kamikaze succeeeded. An Essex class carrier has been struck forward of the island. Curtiss Helldivers as well as Avengers are spotted aft, ready to launch.

Right: An unidentified small freighter under attack by Task Force 58 carrier planes. Bombs have already started a fire amidships and near-misses churn up the water on either side.

Left: Avengers made some of the biggest tonnage hauls of the war in a series of strikes against Japanese fleet bases in July 1945. Here a cruiser is badly mauled in an attack upon Kure Harbour.

Battles of the Philippine Sea

TBF-1s of Composite Squadron 30 off light carrier *Monterey* en route to a strike against Nauru Atoll on 8 December 1943.
/ *R. M. Hill*

The two largest naval battles of World War II were both fought in that wide expanse of the Western Pacific called the Philippine Sea. They came four months apart, involving hundreds of warships and thousands of aircraft. Their like will never be seen again.

The First Battle of the Philippine Sea — better known in aviation circles as 'The Great Marianas Turkey Shoot' — was sparked by the American invasion of Saipan. With Guam and Tinian, Saipan was too valuable for the Japanese to lose if there were to be any hope of stopping the Allied advance. Therefore, the Imperial Navy came out of hiding for the first time in nearly two years. The Japanese dispatched nine carriers and numerous consorts to contest the Saipan landings. The American carrier commander, Vice-Admiral Marc Mitscher, had 15 flattops embarking 900 aircraft, including nearly 200 TBFs and TBMs.

Avengers of Mitscher's Task Force 58 and the escort carrier groups spent the first few days of the campaign in routine chores. Bombing, ground support, anti-sub patrol and reconnaissance. The great air battles of 19 June saw the Hellcat squadrons decimate the Japanese air groups as they struck four times at the fast carrier force. Not till the 20th did Avengers play a larger part in the battle, and then it was crucial.

Two Japanese carriers had been sunk by US submarines, but the remainder were fleeing westward after losing the majority of their planes on the 19th. All through the morning and afternoon of the 20th, TBFs and F6Fs searched for the retreating enemy without success. It appeared the quarry would escape without being brought to battle.

Then at 1540 that afternoon, two search teams from *Enterprise* made contact far to the westward. Each team consisted of two Avengers and a Hellcat — the teams being led by Lt Robert S. Nelson and Lt(jg) Robert R. 'Railroad' Jones. Nelson first noticed a ripple on the horizon slightly to port of his flight path. Rain squalls obscured visibility, but Lt(jg) Ed Laster of Jones' team, also flying a TBF, sighted the enemy fleet a few minutes later, from the adjoining search sector. Therefore, the two *Enterprise* teams approached the hostile fleet from opposite directions. Nelson and Jones were both transmitting the enemy's estimated position and composition to Mitscher within minutes. As Nelson remained in the area to amplify the contact and correct his original report, Jones scooted for the task force, repeating the message over and over. Bob Jones recalled:

'My most vivid recollections of the search flight are of the Japanese carrier leaving a circular wake as it turned after we had been in view of it for four or five minutes while we circled, double-checking the plot of our position.

'As we were returning after transmitting the contact report, I also recall the sight of fighter pilot Ned Colgan's F6F as he swooped down and away in pursuit of the Japanese plane we spotted heading on opposite course, possibly carrying a contact report of its own. The splash of the Jap plane, shot down by Colgan in the distance, was in a way anti-climactic.

'The sight of the outgoing TBFs and other attack planes passing on opposite course high overhead was most impressive, and the most clearly remembered event of the day.'

It was indeed impressive, as nearly 220 planes had been launched from Task Force 58 upon receipt of the Avengers' reports. Among the strike group was a total of 57 Avengers from 10 different carriers. Torpedo One off *Yorktown* contributed the most, with nine TBFs. The *Hornet* and *Bunker Hill* squadrons both launched eight Avengers. Seven took off from *Wasp*, six from *Lexington*, and five from *Enterprise*. Three light carriers — *Belleau Wood*, *Monterey*, and *Cabot* — each put up four. *San Jacinto's* VT-51 launched two torpedo planes. But fewer than 20 of the 57 Avengers were armed with torpedoes. The rest carried bombs.

Five Avengers aborted the mission with various mechanical problems: two each from VT-1 and VT-2, and one from VT-16. That left 52 torpedo bombers to attack the Japanese fleet just as the red sun was setting over the western horizon of the Philippine Sea.

The Japanese had known they would be attacked, and put up as strong a CAP as possible, about 75 planes. Most were Zero fighters but the defenders also included some dive bombers.

Despite the great disparity of numbers, the Japanese pilots proved generally aggressive. Torpedo Two off *Hornet* was the only TBF squadron which was not engaged by Japanese aircraft. The other Avenger units reported attacks by 43 bandits, but the escorting Hellcats took good care of the strike planes. Only two TBF squadrons were molested seriously enough to fire in self-defence. *Enterprise's* VT-10 saw 12 hostiles and two gunners fired at those which came close enough. One Zero fell into the water. But *Lexington's* VT-16 was not so fortunate. Attacked from above and behind by 11 fighters, the score was even at one Zero and one Avenger shot down.

The unfortunate *Lexington* flier was Lt(jg) Warren E. McLellan, the only TBF pilot shot down by an enemy plane over the Japanese fleet. But his luck was not all bad. McLellan

and his two crewmen survived 22 hours in the water before being rescued. He reported upon his return:

'I heard various people say over the radio that Zekes were in the air, and soon afterwards about 50 tracers appeared to pass through my plane and go directly out ahead and slightly upward, as though an enemy fighter was making a run from below and astern. The horizontal stabiliser of the TBF apparently hid the Zeke from the view of my turret gunner because he had been alerted to the presence of enemy fighters ahead and was keeping a careful lookout.

'As soon as the first bullets passed through the plane, I pulled back quickly on the stick to avoid other possible bursts, but a fire started in the cockpit on the port side. The cockpit was ablaze before I could find the microphone. However, the crewmen fortunately realised the gravity of our situation and were ready to parachute almost as soon as I. Leaning out of the cockpit as far as possible, I placed my feet upon the instrument panel and pushed myself out.

'Before pulling my ripcord I waited until I had fallen clear of the area where most of the Japanese planes were and where the heavy anti-aircraft shells were bursting. When the parachute opened, I seemed to be suspended in mid-air, where I was in an excellent position to observe the battle going on around and below me. The attack on a Shokaku class carrier was only about half completed at this time, but I had seen two good bomb hits on her before being attacked by the Zeke, so she must have received considerable damage. However, my attention soon became occupied with trying to see where the bullets were coming from that were passing nearby. Shrapnel was falling in the water all around, and I saw a Zeke strafe an object in the water, which may have been our TBF, almost directly underneath me.

'So much had been happening that I failed to prepare for a water landing until I saw the water coming up to meet me. By working fast, however, I removed most of the parachute harness before hitting the water. Since the buoyancy of my backpack tended to hold me face down in the water, I had to cut one side of the strap. However, I was unable to locate the buckle that fastened the one-man liferaft to the parachute, and as the chute was becoming water-soaked and was almost pulling me under, I was afraid to fasten the raft to my life jacket. My knife was lost in trying to cut the raft from the parachute, and soon the raft was gone, too. The backpack was the only thing saved, and it became water-soaked after about eight hours and had to be abandoned.'

Early the next morning, search planes

dropped liferafts to McLellan and his crew. Late that afternoon they were rescued and returned to *Lexington.*

The Zeke shot down by McLellan's squadron was credited to the turret gunner in the CO's aircraft. AMM1/c J. W. Webb, flying with Lt Norman A. Sterrie, saw the Zeke make a level run from the 0530 position as VT-16 withdrew after its attack. Webb could not depress his .50cal enough to fire during the Zeke's run, but neither did the Japanese score any hits. As the Zeke pulled away, it climbed slightly and Webb fired about 20 rounds into the underside of the fuselage and wingroots. The Mitsubishi began to burn, went into the water at a 45° angle, and exploded.

While only one Avenger was lost to enemy aircraft, three fell to the heavy, multi-coloured flak. Two of *Yorktown's* VT-1 TBFs were shot down, and VT-24 from *Belleau Wood* also sustained a loss to AA fire. But the Torpedo 24 crews obtained the best results.

Air Group 24 launched 12 planes: eight Hellcats and four Avengers. Leading the TBF division was Lt(jg) George P. Brown, with Lt(jg) Warren R. Omark, Benjamin C. Tate, and W. D. Luton. All four TBF-1Cs were armed with torpedoes.

Warren Omark relates the events of that evening:

'Just prior to launching, George Brown made the statement to our skipper that we would get a carrier. I believe the distance was about 300 miles, and it gave us plenty of time to reflect and think about the forthcoming attack.

'The strike group commander led us to the Japanese fleet, and my recollection is that we were at 12,000ft. The enemy fleet was a large task force consisting of carriers, battleships, cruisers and destroyers. The light conditions were still very good at the time, and each squadron from the respective carriers selected the targets that they wanted to attack.

'Brownie had spotted the largest carrier, which of course was well protected by a surrounding screen. Fighters from the *Belleau Wood* were quickly engaged in fighting off attacking Japanese airplanes, so we made the attack on the carrier with no cover. Brownie led us into a rather sharp dive at the Japanese fleet. In so doing, Luton was separated from the division and actually proceeded in an attack on another part of the fleet.'

Though it would not be known for many hours, Luton sighted a light carrier and went after it. He saw his torpedo make a normal water entry and noticed the wake heading toward the target. But in taking evasive action, Luton made a sharp 180° turn and could not observe the result of his attack. Apparently his torpedo missed, as no other Japanese carriers were torpedoed. Flak damage prevented Luton's bomb bay doors from closing, and the additional drag increased his fuel consumption. Flying back towards the task force with four other planes, he ran out of gasoline and made a water landing. Luton and his crew were rescued the next day.

Omark recalls how the attack developed upon the main target:

'Brownie, Ben Tate and I fanned out to approach from different angles. The attack course took us over the outlying screen of destroyers, then cruisers, and finally the battleships. This screen had to be penetrated in order to reach the proper range for launching torpedoes against the carrier. The anti-aircraft fire was very intense and I took as much evasive action as I could to avoid being hit.

'During the attack, Brownie's aircraft was hit by AA fire and caught fire. I think one of the remarkable stories of the war then took place. George Platz and Ellis Babcock were the two crewmen in Brownie's plane, and on knowing their plane was afire and unable to reach Brownie on the intercom, they

parachuted and actually witnessed the attack from the water. They remained there all night and were found and rescued the next day by search planes from our task force.

'We came in at about 400ft from the water to get a satisfactory launch of our torpedoes and dropped them on converging courses which presumably did not allow the enemy carrier to take effective evasive action. Platz and Babcock later reported that we did hit the carrier and that it later sank. It was reported as a Hayataka class CV, but later we understood this was a Hiyo class ship. It was comparable to our own Essex class carriers, but had been converted from a luxury liner before the war.'

This latter information was correct. There was in fact no Hayataka class in the Imperial Navy — probably a translation error by US intelligence. The *Belleau Wood* Avengers attacked *Hiyo* herself, name ship of the class which displaced over 24,000 tons and measured some 720ft overall. Omark continued:

'The TBF I was flying performed just beautifully in this entire attack. Everything functioned as required, and I have nothing but good things to say about the planes manufactured by Grumman. As I retired from this attack, I in turn was pursued and attacked by some Zeros. Again I took evasive action, and we returned fire from our turret gun, and eventually lost the attacking fighters.'

Lt(jg) Ben Tate also had a harrowing experience during the attack upon *Hiyo*:

'George Brown was a very aggressive aviator. He came in on the ship ahead and to the port side and just a few seconds ahead of me on the starboard side. I saw Brown's fish hit the water close in and in perfect position. He dropped on the port side but the carrier was turning through his fish and it would have hit on the starboard side. Brown pulled out to the port side and I lost sight of him flying down the gun mounts on that side.

'At one point I found myself going at 340kts which is near or past the red line. I wanted to drop at 200ft and 200kts, which I did, by pulling the throttle all the way back. I remember feeling rather stupid hearing my wheel warning horn blowing as I flew through the Jap fleet. We had everybody shooting at us.

'As I flew down the side of the carrier I thought I saw tracers in the cockpit. I decided this was delusion until one hit my hand, taking off a few inches of the top of the stick. I retired close to a battleship which fired broadsides into the water in front of me, but when I got to the splashes, there was no effect. I do remember that when the

battleship fired its broadside the whole side of the ship looked red.'

Like Omark, Tate was pursued by Zeros but he evaded them in a cloud layer. Heading towards the rendezvous point, Tate came upon Brown, flying erratically into the gathering darkness. Tate attempted to keep Brown in sight but finally lost track of him and proceeded alone. When the battle-damaged TBF ran out of fuel short of the task force, Tate made a successful water landing. He was rescued next day with his crew by a US destroyer.

Warren Omark's experiences continued to parallel Tate's. Shortly after escaping the vengeful Zeros, Omark also found George Brown:

'Brownie's crewmen had bailed out, and he was alone in the plane. The fire was out but the undersurface was blackened from the flames. The plane had suffered considerable damage. He was flying with the cockpit open,

and it was obvious that he was badly injured himself. He seemed in a very dazed state. It was a tribute to the TBF that it was still flying in spite of this considerable damage, and had Brownie himself not been injured so badly he may have made it back to our fleet. I stayed with him and tried to have him fly on my wing as I started to return. He was in obvious trouble, because he wandered around the sky, and it was with a complete sense of frustration that we knew we could do nothing to help him. Finally as it grew dark he simply wandered off and we could no longer find him. We can only surmise that he fainted and crashed.

'By this time I was completely separated from the other returning planes. It was a long flight back and I did everything possible to conserve fuel. With dead reckoning navigation the course which I took to presumably put me near our task force was obviously wrong. I could not pick up the homing signal which would have given me a

Above: **The Marianas campaign was disastrous for the Japanese Navy. Three carriers were sunk and nearly 400 naval aircraft destroyed on 19-20 June 1944. Here the heavy carrier** *Zuikaku* **is badly damaged and afire while still under attack by US carrier aircraft on the afternoon of the 20th.** *Zuikaku* **survived the damage inflicted by TBFs and SB2Cs, but lived on for only four more months.** / *Grumman*

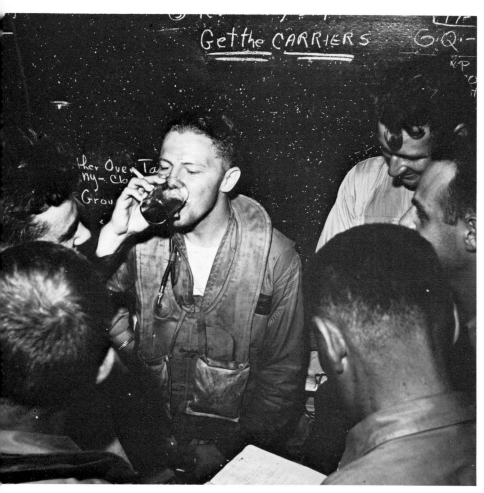

Above: **Lt Don P. Gift enjoys a cigarette and some liquid refreshment in his squadron's ready room after the hectic dusk strike against Japanese carriers on 20 June 1944. Gift was one of 57 Avenger pilots flying the mission, with the objective still written on the blackboard.** / *Grumman*

Luton were safe and that Platz and Babcock had been rescued, but that Brownie was missing. It was then reported that we had sunk the Japanese carrier.'

Hiyo was the only enemy carrier lost in the 200-plane attack. Other carriers were damaged by TBFs, SBDs, and SB2Cs carrying bombs, but the VT-24 trio with its torpedoes claimed the sole success against a combatant vessel. A pair of Japanese fleet oilers was sunk by the *Wasp* air group, but otherwise the Imperial Navy escaped from the Marianas without further loss.

In exchange, nearly half of the 220 American aircraft launched on the dusk strike were lost. Only about 20 were attributed to enemy action; the majority either splashed down out of fuel or were wrecked in landing accidents. The TBF and TBM casualties were typical: four shot down over the Japanese fleet and 25 lost to operational causes. This amounted to 50% of the torpedo bombers which took off to strike the Japanese carriers. But efficient rescue work kept American aircrew losses to fewer than 50 pilots and crewmen. It could have been much worse.

The Second Battle of the Philippine Sea, like the first, was better known by another name. More frequently this widespread naval-air conflict has been called the Battle of Leyte Gulf, for it was conducted as a result of General Douglas MacArthur's promised return to the Philippines. It was also the last major fleet engagement ever fought, lasting three days.

Perhaps the single largest aerial torpedo action of the war occurred in the Sibuyan Sea on 24 October 1944. Japanese Admiral Kurita's powerful surface force of five battleships, 13 cruisers and 15 destroyers was headed for San Bernardino Strait to contest the amphibious landings on the east coast of Leyte. US submarines sank two cruisers on the 23rd, but still the armada continued east. The skipper of *Franklin's* torpedo squadron, Lt-Cdr Larry French, tells what happened:
'On 23 October, reports started to filter in of Japanese fleet units on the move toward the Philippines. On the 24th two large groups of heavy warships were spotted closing on Leyte from different directions. We waited anxiously all that morning for further information on their positions. Finally, about 1500 word came. "Pilots man your planes. Target: Japanese fleet in the Sibuyan Sea."'

Carrier strikes had been in progress since mid-morning, but as French relates:
'There were other US carrier task groups in the area, but the groups were not co-ordinated. Our attack was to be a combined

vector to the fleet, and it was at this time that I broke radio silence, and called the *Belleau Wood*, asking for a vector.

'The task force had night fighters in the air, which I was not aware of, and sent one of them out to find me. And he did just that. I can recall what a great sense of relief it was to suddenly see this F6F night fighter flying off my wing. He brought me back to the fleet, then separated, and to this day I have no idea who that pilot was. But it is with a considerable amount of gratitude that I talk about this part of the story.

'Since there were a considerable number of planes in the air, and it was dark, Admiral Mitscher had made a decision for the ships to turn on their lights. Again, I can recall what a fantastic sight that was in seeing the lights from the task force. It was a remarkable beacon.

'I landed on the first carrier I could find. I remember advising my two crewmen prior to landing to be prepared as any minute we might run out of gas and have to land in the water. When we caught that wire aboard the *Lexington*, my crewmen let out a very expressive cry of joy. The flight had been well over five hours.

'We remained overnight and were launched next day to return to *Belleau Wood*. There we learned that Ben Tate and bombing-torpedo attack, and the *Franklin* strike contained 24 dive bombers, about 12 fighter escorts, and 10 TBMs with ring-tail torpedoes. The group proceeded on a west-northwest course at 17,000ft across Samar Island to the Sibuyan Sea — a distance of 250 miles. No enemy fighters were sighted and visibility at the target was good.

'On arriving at the scene I observed that two groups of Japanese ships were already in their air defence and steaming in circles. This would present some problems for a torpedo attack against these heavy fleet units. We would attack two target groups simultaneously, hoping to get a shot off the bow of a heavy ship as it was coming around. Our formation approached from the east, with half the bombers and torpedo planes going for battleships to the south and half towards heavy ships to the north.'

Part of the reason the Japanese armada was scattered was that the giant battleship *Musashi* had been previously damaged and was lagging behind her sister *Yamato*. But both super dreadnoughts retained heavy

Below: A TBM-1D of *San Jacinto's* VT-51 on patrol near the Marianas in 1944. / *R. M. Hill*

Bottom: Four TBF-1C and TBM-1C aircraft of Torpedo Squadron 15, operating off USS *Essex* in mid-July 1944. Air Group 15 was one of the few formations to fly in both battles of the Philippine Sea; the first in June and the second in October. / *R. M. Hill*

Top: **This TBM-1 belongs to VC-11 aboard escort carrier *Nehenta Bay*, flying over Tinian on 25 July 1944.** / *R. M. Hill*

defensive screens composed of cruisers and destroyers, not to mention three lesser battleships. French continues:

'The SB2Cs moved over the targets at 18,000ft and commenced dive bombing. The torpedo planes came straight in from the side, right at the circling ships, descending from 4,000ft and arriving at the release point as the last bombs were striking. During the high-speed approach the AA fire was very heavy. The battleships were even firing their main batteries at us. Not directly at the planes; but to lay down a salvo in the water in front of us. The shell splashes would send up a high column of water, thus hoping a plane would fly into it. I learned these tactics

back in VT-5 on the old *Yorktown* before the war. Thus I wasn't surprised, but it sure could pop your Mark 8 eyeballs!

'These salvoes were ineffective against the torpedo attack, as we were approaching the release point at about 260kts and 600-800ft. Our objective was to shoot across the ship's bow as it came around toward us. We did get in and all fired, but it was almost impossible to be at the proper range as the ship came by.

'My first and second divisions claimed four possible hits. Two were on the biggest battleship, the *Musashi*, one was on a cruiser, and the possible additional hit reported I did not see. The third and fourth divisions got a hit on a cruiser of the northern group. We lost two TBMs shot down by the thick AA fire and had one plane return with heavy damage.'

In all, six US air groups struck the Kurita force during the day in a series of attacks. Some pilots flew two missions as *Intrepid, Cabot, Lexington, Essex, Franklin* and *Enterprise* flung successive strikes at the armada. It was a long, dangerous, tiring business, but it accomplished results. *Musashi*, at 64,000 tons one of the two largest battleships ever built, succumbed to 19 torpedoes and sank in the Sibuyan Sea the evening of the 24th. Heavy cruiser *Myoko* was so heavily damaged by bombs and torpedoes that she had to turn back. It was carrier airpower's first great victory over battleships manoeuvring in open water. And it would not be the last.

After an all-day pummelling, Kurita was expected to abandon his mission. In fact, scout planes informed Third Fleet commander William F. Halsey that the Sibuyan Sea force was last seen retiring westward. But not for long. Determined to follow orders, the Japanese admiral reversed course and unknown to the Americans resumed his journey toward San Bernardino Strait. He passed through the narrow passage that night with four battleships, eight cruisers, and 11 destroyers.

When this powerful force emerged from the strait early on the morning of the 25th, the Japanese expected easy prey among the almost defenceless transports and amphibious craft of the Leyte invasion fleet. But as Kurita steamed south towards Leyte he encountered a small escort carrier group off the east coast of Samar. This was Taffy Three, six baby flattops with escorting destroyers under the command of Rear Admiral Clifton Sprague.

Taffy Three was in no position to fight so formidable a surface force. The escort carriers had never been intended for a fleet engagement. They were equipped and trained primarily for tactical air support of ground troops, and to provide anti-submarine protection. Hence, the six CVEs' 70-odd Avengers were armed mainly with bombs and depth charges; the 90-plus

Above left, above and right: First to land on each of three islands were Avengers from escort carriers during mid-1944. (*Above left*) The first US aircraft to land at Saipan was this TBM-1C of VC-4 off *White Plains* during June. (*Above*) On 29 July this Avenger became the first American plane to use Orote Field on Guam. (*Right*) Though previously identified as a Marine aircraft, in fact this TBM-1CP belonged to VC-75 off *Ommaney Bay*. It put down on Palau four days after Marines went ashore during September.
/ R. M. Hill; IWM; R. M. Hill

A TBM-1 over Guam on D-Day, 20 July 1944. This escort carrier Avenger provides protection for the first wave of Marines to land on the beach. Besides bombing Japanese installations, CVE planes called in artillery and naval gunfire, flew anti-submarine patrol, and informed ground forces of enemy troop dispositions. / *Grumman*

Wildcats had little more than their four .50cal machine guns.

Ensign Hans Jensen, a TBM pilot on anti-sub patrol north of Taffy Three, flashed the first warning shortly before 0700. He radioed Clifton Sprague and informed him that the distinctive pagoda masts of Japanese battleships were visible. Radar shortly confirmed Jensen's sighting.

Sprague was caught in a most unenviable situation. He could not hope to outdistance his faster opponents, and he certainly could not trade broadsides with them. The largest guns in his force were 5.38-inchers — a poor match for Kurita's battleships and cruisers which mounted everything from 6-inch to 18-inch guns. So Sprague did the only thing he could do. He headed south towards distant help of other escort groups, ordered his ships to lay a smokescreen, and began launching his TBMs and FMs. Many were unarmed.

One of the Avenger pilots who played a prominent role in this uneven battle was Lt-Cdr Ed Huxtable. As commanding officer of Composite Squadron 10 aboard *Gambier Bay,* Huxtable had a bird's eye view of the proceedings:

'I was in the wardroom waiting to get some breakfast when suddenly the general alarm sounded. I thought to myself, here is another hop to the Sulu Sea, and was determined to get a piece of toast and some juice before going to the ready room when my personnel officer came running in, saying, "You'd better get up to the ready room in a hurry. They are already manning the planes." We made for the ready room at a full run.

'As I entered the ready room, Vereen Bell the squadron intelligence officer was there with a flight harness on. As I grabbed my harness and strapped it on I told Vereen, "You better stay here," as I still thought we were headed for the Sulu Sea. I grabbed my plotting board and ran for the flight deck.

'I got in my plane and asked Jerry Gutzweiler, my plane captain, if I had a bomb load. He said no, so I told him to call Buzz Borries, the air officer, if I had time to get a load. We had not turned up the engines as yet and I couldn't see any use going off without some ordnance. I saw Borries move forward and speak to Captain Viewig, who made a sweeping forward motion with his arm as if he were saying, "Get 'em off."

'About this time I was startled by what seemed a rifle shot next to my left ear. I looked and saw that it was a salvo of heavy calibre stuff splashing alongside the *White Plains.* Until this moment I had no idea the enemy was so near. Now I was more than ready to get on that catapult. We turned up engines and three TBMs launched ahead of me. As I shot off, the lead plane had started

his 180° turn for a regular carrier joinup. The ceiling was low at about 1,200ft. After I took the lead I called Admiral Sprague's code name Bendix and asked what our orders were. They came back in an excited voice, "Attack immediately."

'We were headed aft with relation to the ship, and the visibility being poor, I could just see the destroyer plane guards and shortly broke out into better visibility and higher ceilings where I spotted four cruisers near and what appeared to be four battleships further back in the gloom. At this moment the cruisers bearing from our force would be off the port quarter and our force was on an easterly course. There was no possibility of making a high-altitude attack, so I turned back over the destroyers and our carriers, and turned on a course I figured would bring us out over the Jap cruisers. I pulled up into the ceiling and started for the cruisers. What loads the other planes had I did not know, but at least we would give the Japs a scare.

'Suddenly we broke into the clear again on the starboard side of the cruisers which were in line, and red balls of anti-aircraft fire were coming at us in what seemed torrents, but passing just below. I broke to the left and started for the after cruiser in a shallow dive doing about 190kts. The other planes had picked their own targets. When I got to within 3,000yds range the AA fire was getting too hot and I couldn't see being a hero without a bomb load, so I turned left and pulled out aft. I made a wide circle to the left, passing ahead of the cruiser column and come in on their starboard side abeam, paralleling them and watching for their next move.

'I thought I was far enough out at 3,000-4,000yd so they wouldn't shoot at me. Then five different coloured five-inch bursts appeared about 150yd in front of me and I ran through the smoke of the middle burst.

'About this time I called Bendix and suggested that his best course was south. I came back over the carriers and called the *Gambier Bay*. The ship answered and suggested that we go to Tacloban to arm and refuel. But I doubted they had anything there, and I thought we could do more good just harassing the Japanese. The carriers had come into the clear again, and at this time Bill Gallagher joined up on me with his engine smoking. He had launched after I did and made a torpedo attack. I told him to head for the beach and he turned off. Another pilot reported that he saw Bill make a water landing, but Bill and his crew were never recovered.

'After returning to the vicinity of the cruisers, this time on their starboard beam, I saw the third cruiser take a hit aft on the starboard side of the fantail and turn to the left out of formation. She made a complete 360° turn and came in aft of the last cruiser, but slowed down. Shortly thereafter I made a dummy run on the lead cruiser from ahead, and temporarily hiding in the broken overcast, I made another run from the starboard bow. I made the pullouts with the bomb bay doors open, to feign a torpedo drop.

'I flew back toward the carriers and saw that one of them was listing to port and slowed. According to the axis position I thought this was the *White Plains*, but in all the manoeuvring the axis rotation must have shifted, for it was the *Gambier Bay*. The Jap cruisers had closed to about 10,000yd on the carriers and at this point I made another dummy run on the lead cruiser. I fired my .50cal (which were all I had) at an elevated angle in hopes of straddling the target.

'I circled around to the port side of the cruiser line again and they were now under a low overcast. I was at about 1,000ft and between 5,000-6,000yd away. As I was watching, a TBM completely afire fell in the wake of the last cruiser about 200yd astern. I knew that there must be planes above, probably from Taffy Two, so I decided to head for the beach and see if there was any chance of getting a bomb load. This was around 0900.

'After arriving over Tacloban airfield I joined up with six circling TBMs and circled for about 20min as the fighters were getting priority to land since they were getting very low on gas. I decided to go back to the ships and as a group all planes headed back off Samar. When we arrived there were five carriers but no destroyers. They said they could not take us aboard as they were too shot up, so back we went to Tacloban. After circling for awhile, the command ship sent us down to Dulag where we landed shortly after noon.

'Here we could get gas but no bombs. There was a ground controller on the field and we stood by while they decided what they wanted us to do. Finally around 1500 they told us to return to the carriers. We took off and followed the ZB radio signals till we found the ships about 150 miles east in Leyte Gulf. And now there were only four. The *St Lo* had taken a Kamikaze shortly after we left them earlier in the day. But they couldn't take us aboard!

'Now I knew we were in a jackpot, trying to get back to Dulag over Leyte Gulf, for our forces would be shooting at anything in the air. I decided to skirt the south end of the gulf and come north up the coast to Dulag. As we arrived close to the field inland from the Dulag landing site, I saw the ships shoot down a TBM in flames. My only thought was to get on the ground in a hurry. We went into a quick right echelon and broke off to land. My exec was riding with me, for his plane had been hit in the right horizontal stabiliser with what appeared to be a 40mm shell, and we had left it behind. He probably wondered what I was doing when I put the wheels on the grass of that short strip, doing about 120kts with the brakes on, but she skidded to a nice stop at the end of the field. We spent an exciting night with the army at Dulag.

'It was there that I definitely found out that the *Gambier Bay* was gone.'

Another TBM pilot in the air over Taffy Three was Lt(jg) Norm Johnson of VC-68 off *Fanshaw Bay*. His experiences were similar to Huxtable's, but with one important difference. Johnson's Avenger had four 500lb bombs.

'Climbing at full throttle, I penetrated the lower cloud cover and levelled off at 11,000ft. There, I took a final look at the enemy disposition and decided to attack the main force which was firing at the American ships. The latter were steaming at full speed trying to get sea room away from the confinement of Samar Island

'About five miles away, I nosed down to pick up speed. The Japanese battle force at that moment was occupied in anti-aircraft protection against an air attack. Varied coloured bursts mushroomed at several levels. It was quite dense and something I had to penetrate. Bomb bay doors remained closed as speed increased. By that time, three large battleships had entered a circle with rudders hard over and guns spitting flame. At 7,000ft I pushed over into my attack,

Right: The flak-damaged wing-tip of a VT-51 Avenger attests to the accuracy of Japanese AA fire during air strikes on 25 October 1944. Clearly visible are an Ise class battleship and a destroyer, off the north-east coast of Luzon. Further south, off Samar, another Japanese force surprised several American escort carriers due to clever use of the northern force as a decoy. / *National Archives*

Below: Final moments of the Japanese carrier *Zuikaku*, last survivor of the six which launched against Pearl Harbor. The distinctive Avenger silhouette is appropriate, for torpedo-packing TBFs were largely responsible for sinking *Zuikaku* in the Battle of Leyte Gulf on 25 October. Three other Japanese carriers were destroyed in this same action. / *Grumman*

selecting the lead battleship for my target. The interphone from the radioman reminded, "Open bomb bay doors!" I pushed the lever and the doors opened. The immediate drag was apparent as the aircraft was barrelling along by now. Bombs were armed.

'Intent on adjusting the target properly in my sight, the plane corkscrewed and suddenly the right side of the canopy peeled off. I pressed the bomb release button at what seemed the best altitude and concentrated all effort on pulling out of the dive. It was a close call as the aircraft recovered about 50-100ft above the water. The target was so large in my sight that the bombs couldn't miss. I pulled the aeroplane up sharply to avoid further AA fire, and just in case there were enemy fighters around, I took cover in the lower cloud layer.

'The *Fanshaw Bay* had been hit by surface fire, and aircraft aloft were instructed to proceed to Tacloban airfield on the island of Leyte. Just then the Japanese force broke off the engagement and steamed north. The sturdy TBM touched down on a rough runway and braked to a halt one foot from a bomb crater. A ground crewman signalled cut engine. Inspection of the aircraft produced a surprise. Practically every inspection plate had blown off! But even with these missing plates and canopy, the aircraft remained flyable. Later, a non-flyable TBM was found and much-needed parts were cannibalised.

'At dawn the next day, I gave up my foxhole to the army engineers, relieved that an expected banzai charge had not materialised. Soon my TBM and I were headed east to land on the wet deck of an alternate carrier, where we belonged.'

The lopsided battle off Samar should have ended in the annihilation of Taffy Three. Instead, the exceptionally determined attacks by Sprague's aircraft and destroyers, backed up by planes from Taffy Two, forced the Japanese battle squadron to retire. Gunfire had sunk *Gambier Bay* and three US destroyers, and *St Lo* was destroyed by a Kamikaze. But three of Kurita's fast cruisers had been crippled and left behind to sink — largely by the efforts of TBM bombs and torpedos. The threat to MacArthur's invasion force was over.

But the battle was not ended. Kurita had nearly destroyed Taffy Three because Admiral Halsey's fast carriers were far to the north, pursuing the Japanese 'bait' group off Cape Engano. Knowing the Americans could not resist carrier targets, Japan's four active flattops were sacrificed in order to give Kurita the opening he needed in Leyte Gulf. In four major air strikes during the 25th, the air groups of Task Force 38 deprived the Imperial Navy of most of its remaining carriers. Avenger squadrons played a major role in this action, helping sink four carriers and a destroyer. The most successful strike was conducted by Air Groups 19 and 44 off *Lexington* and *Langley* respectively. During the third attack of the day, TBMs of VT-19 and VT-44 put three torpedoes into the already-damaged *Zuikaku*. This finished the veteran of every carrier battle except Midway, and last survivor of the Pearl Harbor strike force. Light carrier *Zuiho* was sunk by elements of five air groups shortly thereafter.

Never again would the Japanese Imperial Navy put to sea with hope of victory.

Above: The 11,200 ton light carrier *Zuiho*, sunk by Avengers and Helldivers in the 25 October 1944 strikes off Cape Engano, Luzon. *Zuiho* has taken hits in her flight deck, visible along the centre line.

Right: The 13,000 ton heavy cruiser *Nachi* under air attack in Manila Bay on 5 November 1944. Avengers and Helldivers scored numerous hits, causing the Myoko class ship to sink stern first. / *Grumman/INS*

Left: Aircrew of VT-51 discuss the results of a strike against the Japanese fleet upon return to light carrier *San Jacinto* on 25 October. / *National Archives*

Avenger by Night

Perhaps the greatest irony of the Avenger's career is that its debut in the night-flying role was as a fighter instead of a bomber.

By late 1943, when the fast carrier task force was pursuing the Pacific War, the need for carrier-based nocturnal protection was evident. The US Navy had made its carrier decks almost immune to daylight air attack, but Japanese bombers were largely free to harass the flattops by night.

The *Enterprise* air group commander thought he had a way to correct the situation. He was Lt-Cdr Edward H. O'Hare, veteran fighter pilot and an advocate of carrier-based night operations. O'Hare reasoned that a radar-equipped TBF could guide a pair of conventional F6F Hellcats to successful interceptions at night, and convinced his superiors to let him try.

During the invasion of the Gilbert Islands in November 1943, O'Hare worked out a plan with Lt-Cdr John C. Phillips, skipper of Torpedo Squadron 6 aboard *Enterprise*. Shipboard radar would detect hostile aircraft approaching at long range and vector the TBF and two F6Fs within range of the Avenger's airborne set. Then Phillips' radar operator would assume the contact and put one or both fighters on to the hostile aircraft.

The radar officer was Lt(jg) H. B. Rand, an electronics specialist from Massachussetts Institute and Technology. He was among the early graduates of the Navy Radar School, and would play an important part in this early experiment.

Shortly before sunset on 26 November, task force radar detected unidentified aircraft approaching. O'Hare and his wingman launched first, hopeful of making contact with some daylight remaining, and Phillips followed in his Avenger. As darkness fell, Rand got a good blip on his scope and steered the TBF towards a bogey at 1,200ft. The range closed to one mile, and Phillips identified the intruder as a Betty bomber. Firing his two wing .50cals, he shot down the Mitsubishi from astern as his turret gunner A. B. Kernan also fired. Almost immediately the night sky was criss-crossed with a sparkling pattern of tracer shells. In the surprise and confusion, nearby Bettys were shooting at one another. Kernan returned fire at some of the nearer gun flashes, but no results were observed. However, the flames of the destroyed Betty were seen by O'Hare and he led his wingman towards the scene to rejoin formation.

The CAG asked Phillips to turn on his lights for an easier rendezvous, but at that moment the TBF's radar scope glowed with another contact. Down to 500ft, he followed the Betty through a gentle turn, firing continuously. This bomber splashed down in what appeared to be a controlled water landing. Phillips had made two kills in two contacts.

O'Hare and his wingman then moved into formation with the TBF, showing their navigation lights. Kernan in the Avenger turret fired at two silhouettes which resembled blacked-out aircraft during the join-up, and shortly thereafter the lead Hellcat dropped from view. Extensive searches and debriefing failed to provide any conclusive evidence of Butch O'Hare's mysterious disappearance.

The death of so popular and respected an officer as O'Hare caused substantial discussion within naval aviation. But it was undeniable that the improvised 'bat team' had successfully broken up a large nocturnal air attack on the task force. The concept was proven, and from then on radar-equipped F6Fs operated on their own without reliance upon 'seeing-eye' Avengers.

Nocturnal bombing by carrier aircraft was made a reality in large part by the persistence and determination of one man: William I. Martin, a 'trade-school lieutenant during the early days of the war', according to one of his *Enterprise* pilots, Charles E. Henderson, III.

As Henderson recalled:
'Bill Martin was famous because of two things: "On the Road to Douglas County", which he would render enthusiastically given the slightest encouragement (apparently it was "a long and teed-jus jurnee" to his home in the Missouri outback) and for his obsession with the feasability of night operations off a carrier deck. Clearly he was demented.'

Martin had flown one tour aboard *Enterprise* as executive officer in Scouting Squadron 10 in 1942. Thus, his early experience was in SBDs, but he also liked the TBF. He recalls:

'I'd heard that radar was being installed in TBFs. I realised that night flying would give a new dimension to carrier air groups if they could do their business at night, and if they weren't held down in weather. Also, I'd almost spun myself in a couple of times, and I was determined that I was going to be a good instrument pilot.'

Henderson takes up the story from there:

'Bill and a lowly jg named Henry Loomis would regularly sneak off with Scoofer Coffin's TBF during periods when the air group was resting at Espiritu Santo. Scoofer's TBF probably had the only airborne radar set in the SW Pacific. Scoofer commanded VT-10 but was fully occupied and he couldn't have cared less.

'So Bill and Henry, our first fleet airborne radar expert who had brought the gear with him, played games. They demonstrated that they could search and find ships at over 35 miles (eventually 50) and that they could make successful minimum altitude attacks on ships in the dirtiest weather, at night.'

When Martin returned to the States with Air Group 10 in the spring of 1943, he was slated for duty as an instructor. That was the last thing he wanted. He reflects:

'So when I went back to the States, I managed to be "sick" each time they wanted to put me in a primary training squadron, and I remained "sick" until an opening was available in an instrument squadron.

'So I volunteered to get into TBFs, because they did have radar, and my next assignment was to command VT-10. The squadron was reforming at NAS Seattle, and we began to specialise in night flying. My

argument to the staff people, who said we were supposed to do this sort of thing in daytime, was that it would be twice as valuable at night. And I had a bunch of kids who were willing to do it. So we flew at night around San Point and over to Pasco in eastern Washington. Then we went to Hawaii and really concentrated on it, so that's why VT-10 had an extra dimension in its capability.'

Henderson was one of the VT-10 pilots from the first tour who 'stayed on, as we were intrigued'. He relates some of the factors involved in this top-rated mission:

'Protected by a young, aggressive admiral named Arthur Radford, first at Sand Point and then on Maui, Bill drove us hard. Nothing but instruments and night operations. Then at Maui we did long night searches and attacks against friendly ships. As our skills developed we improved our equipment. Bill's imagination fired us with innovation. We regrouped our instruments, developed indirect red lighting, an alarm buzzer on our radio altimeters to prevent us from flying into the water, and a night gunsight. Our new TBFs, when they came, had a .50cal gun in each wing.

'What we couldn't requisition, we stole. "Turkey" Henderson, Aviation Mechanic Third Class, was the principal requisitioner from my engineering department. He ranged from one end of the Hawaiian Islands to the other in his private TBF which we provided him. He never failed. Despite the most blatant offences, he was never caught. No one was safe: Army, Navy, or Marines!'

The intensive training and practice proved worthwhile, as Martin relates:

'We were really ready when we went aboard *Enterprise*, and I think the classic was the Truk raid of 16 February 1944. But a week before that, I broke my left elbow while exercising aboard ship. The doctor put a full cast on it, and it took almost three weeks for it to heal.

'In the meantime, Admiral Mitscher had approved this night attack on Truk, and I wasn't able to lead it. But the squadron was so well trained that it really wasn't necessary for me to be there. Van Eason led the mission, and used what we called our standard attack. You pick an initial point, and the planes go in a couple of minutes apart, and then come back out to a rendezvous point for return to the carrier. This gives you some mutual support and mutual navigation.

'Our 12 planes went in there, looking for Japanese shipping, and each one had four 500lb bombs. They all made four passes, and they weren't going to waste any of them. Our normal attack was at 250ft and about

Left: **Cdr William I. Martin, the leading advocate and practitioner of night carrier operations. Martin probably holds the US record for nocturnal deck landings — nearly 150 in SBD dive bombers and over 210 in Avengers and Hellcats.** / *National Archives*

Above: **The TBF-1D was among the first of all night-flying Avenger variants.** / *R. M. Hill*

150kts indicated, so we could maintain a steady altitude. We had this procedure that when your target disappeared under your nose, you'd count "One alligator two" and pickle a bomb, and you'd hit the waterline of a ship almost every time. Since the bombs had a slight delay, they would penetrate the hull of a merchant ship and let the plane pass over before the explosion. Then you'd change your course and start jinking to avoid AA fire.

'Anyway, our planes achieved surprise and picked their targets carefully. There was a hospital ship in there which we didn't want to hit, and we had pretty good intelligence on where it was. I believe the 12 planes got 13 Japanese ships that were sunk or beached, and we lost one TBF. I'm told the Japanese confirmed after the war that our estimate of damage inflicted was accurate. The great thing, though, was that half of our bombs were hits that night. It was more than you normally get during a daytime attack, with attendant higher losses.'

Greatly encouraged, Martin urged formation of a full-time night air group. At a time when night fighters were being criticised for disrupting a task group's nocturnal routine and being of questionable value, most staff officers and aviators were enthusiastic about the concept of night bombing. Upon return to the US, Martin began forming Night Air Group 90, which reported aboard *Enterprise* at the end of 1944. It seemed that whenever there was any night flying to be done from carriers, the Big E was involved.

But Martin's was actually the second night air group in the US Navy, as Air Group 41 had become operational aboard the light carrier *Independence* that autumn. The Avenger squadron was VT(N)-41 under Lt William R. Taylor, who had formed his unit as a detachment of Lt-Cdr Turner Caldwell's VF(N)-79. In August 1944 79 Fighting was

reorganised into the two squadrons of Night Air Group 41 with Caldwell as the air group commander.

Taylor's TBM-1Ds had the ASD-1 radar which possessed a 40-mile search capability. But the air group was poorly used in its first months of combat, being relegated largely to conventional daytime operations. As a result, up till the end of 1944 the *Independence* TBMs sank only one ship and damaged six others. But Cdr Caldwell's squadrons demonstrated that a night carrier was useful and desirable, and three other nocturnal air groups would see combat before the war ended.

The most successful of these was Bill Martin's Air Group 90. With considerable experience and experimentation to draw upon, the later night fliers entered combat with much-improved equipment and training. Martin describes some of the changes:

'We felt that at night we weren't going to get shot down by anti-aircraft fire, and certainly not by Japanese fighters. Since the TBM gunners weren't needed at night, we tried to get all the defensive stuff taken out, including armour plate, except one plate behind the pilot. We figured that by removing the turret we saved about 1,500lb of unnecessary weight, and we took out the .30cal stinger in the belly. With this weight saving we could put two big fuel tanks in the bomb bay and still have ordnance in other half. By this time we were also able to carry five-inch rockets under the wings, so we had a pretty good ordnance load and also enough fuel to go a lot further.

'The pilot had a radar scope in his cockpit but the main search set was in the belly, facing forward with two operators. We found we needed two men to spell each other, because on a long mission after about 20min of looking at the radar, your eyes could get fatigued.

'Our requests to get these aircraft modified were repeatedly turned down. So with about 10 days to go, as I recall, I flew over to see the highest level possible at Ford Island, and got all the way up to Admiral Towers. He told me, "Our aeronautical engineers have studied this thing, and the aeroplane won't fly the way you want to use it." What he didn't know was that we had worked all night before in VT(N)-90 to do the modification. So I told Admiral Towers, "If it won't fly sir, I request a jeep to take me back to Barbers Point because I flew a modified TBM over here, and if it won't fly, I sure don't want to fly it back."

'He laughed about it, and we all went to have a look at the aeroplane. As it turned out, we had moved the centre of gravity very far forward; we had a hard time getting the tail

down. But we corrected that by putting 20lb or so of lead in the tail, which moved the centre of gravity back where it was a flying machine again.

'But even with our weight saving, we still had the trouble of settling off the bow of the carrier on take-off, or even with a catapult launch. It could be exciting in daytime, but at night when you feel the plane settling under you and you have to rely on the surface effect to sustain lift, it calls for a lot of experience and lots of confidence.

'Navigation was another problem. When you left the carrier you had what was called Point Option, where the carrier was supposed to be when you got back. But with a threatened attack or normal changes it wasn't unusual for Point Option to be up to 80 miles from where it was briefed. We paid

Left: **The US Navy's first full-time night air group was Air Group 41, aboard the light carrier *Independence* from September 1944 to January 1945. Here, a VT(N)-41 TBM-1D taxies into catapult position for launch on 10 October 1944.**
/ R. M. Hill

Above: Another night Avenger was the TBM-3E. The E variants used APS-4 radar, which was best employed in seeking surface targets at close range. / *R. M. Hill*

a lot of attention to the wind from the state of the sea, by judging whitecaps when flying low. And most of our night flying was done at low level. You could be quite accurate, within two or three knots, by estimating wind force from the sea state.

'At this time we had the YE-ZB homer, but it was of limited use. It would give you an approximate bearing, but no range information at all. You could fly a timed triangle to determine the distance, but it was only approximate. So largely we had to rely on our dead reckoning navigation. One big advantage we had over the day air groups was that we could use our search radar in the TBMs to locate the task force in darkness or bad weather. But here again, we were relatively limited because the World War II radars could seldom scan beyond straight line of sight.

'To do this we would pop up to 1,500ft for a look-see and then drop right down again, because you don't want to give away the position of your force or your aircraft, either.

'For getting back aboard ship, we used an idea of Turner Caldwell from the *Independence.* By putting an aircraft radar on the deck edge of the carrier, the ship could tell a pilot if he was too close or too far out in his timed turn to approach the deck. If the pilot had made a precision turn in the pattern, he would be able to see a bright amber light on the quarter of the carrier. It was hooded so it was only visible from the correct spot in the approach pattern. Then when a pilot saw that light, he knew he could start his turn in toward the flight deck. And at that time he could probably leave his instruments and pick up the ship and the landing signal officer visually. So the initial approach was made at 150ft with a slow let-down till you got visual contact at 125ft.

'Night vision was very important, of course. We used indirect red lighting in the ready room and in the aircraft cockpits. We even had red lighting for our flashlights. You took every precaution you could to avoid losing your night visibility.'

Night Air Group 90 retained 17 personnel from Martin's old VT-10. The fighters were 34 F6F-5Ns or -5Es while the bomber squadron, under Lt Russell Kippin, operated 27 TBM-3Ds. The Avengers performed a variety of duties, including night strike, search, heckler missions and electronics warfare such as seeking enemy radio and radar frequencies.

Among Kippin's pilots was Charlie Henderson, who found that his radar could get him both in and out of trouble.

'We harassed about Tokyo Bay in murky, icy rain and pitch dark while Henry Loomis pinpointed radar installations with his new toys. On the way home he spotted an aircraft on his scope. Off we went, helter-skelter. Much later we lost the enemy; likewise ourselves. I had no idea within 100 miles of our position. And no homer at base; it had been secured due to intense enemy activity. More by luck than good management we chanced within radar range of the task force. Henry brought us home.

'But where was the "Big E"? 120 ships covered an area 30 or 40 miles across. During the night as he launched and landed aircraft, Rear-Admiral Matt Gardner and his TG-58.5 would charge from one end to the other of this endless flotilla, to their considerable annoyance. No wonder the senior admirals made us sit on the deck!

'119 ships teeming with eager, trigger-happy gunners! We had to fly for miles to get around them. We landed with sighs of relief and barely enough fuel to taxi down the deck. We also landed with a fresh mission. Air to air intercepts were feasible with our TBMs. But we needed lots of practice.'

Eight Unfriendlies
Charles English Henderson III

From 1942 to 1945, TBFs and TBMs were credited with 98 Japanese aircraft shot down in aerial combat. Three-quarters of these were claimed by carrier-based Navy Avengers while land-based Navy and Marine squadrons accounted for the other 26. Against this, 20 carrier-based Avengers were known lost to Japanese fighters from 1943 to 1945.

The most successful Avenger pilot against enemy aircraft was Lt Charles E. Henderson, III. In two combat tours aboard *Enterprise*, with Torpedo Squadron 10 and Night Torpedo Squadron 90, he experienced eight encounters with airborne hostiles or unidentified aircraft. And in those eight encounters he shot down four Japanese aircraft; a Jake, a Jill, an Emily and a Rufe. It was an exceptional feat of airmanship. Charlie Henderson missed becoming an ace by one victory — in a torpedo plane. But his first combat was an inauspicious one.

'It was a beautiful Pacific morning with high floating cumulus. The rising sun glinted on the tight air group formation floating above the milky clouds. 16 February 1944. Our first strike against the Pacific bastion of another Rising Sun, Truk Atoll.

'After my dive-bombing run on a ship in the central harbour, I headed back across the atoll to our rendezvous at the coral outer reef. Cutting across my bow was a small seaplane, heading for base. It was too much of a temptation, with my two splendid new .50cal wing guns finally wrested from the clutches of BuAer. But 250kts did not close him fast enough, as he spotted me and darted for safety. Clever fellow, I thought; he was luring me into a line of anti-aircraft guns. He was at extreme range but it was my only chance, as tracers began to flash past. Two long bursts. He smoked. But my ammunition was exhausted. Also my nerve. I broke off. And none too soon, as the AA fire became intense.

'Furious with myself for muffing it, I headed again for our rendezvous. As I approached the outer reef, an Avenger trailing smoke slanted out of the sun, a Zero riding its tail. The TBF was a sitting duck; but a tail shot is no easy matter, as the Zero was learning.

'Why didn't the TBF evade? Perhaps he was remembering earlier instructions: provide a stable platform for your turret.

'My wing guns were dry so I called my gunner and said, "I'm going to put you alongside that Zero, and he's all yours, son".

'And I did. But Daniel Boone in this finest hour couldn't have hit anything with that bloody turret. It was like using pistols — for James Bond and the movies only. I did accomplish one thing, though. I made the Zero pilot mad as hell. He forgot all about poor old Bob Jones, smoking lustily by this time. Jonesy got home thanks to his tenacity and a very rugged aircraft.

'The Zero pulled up gracefully in a high chandelle, in the lead, perfectly positioned for a high side run. Having considered such an eventually, as I dreamed of one day becoming a fighter pilot, I had decided upon the tactics I would employ. As he spiralled upwards, I dived at 45° to his track. As he peeled off for his first run, I pulled up and around until we were on opposite courses. When I estimated firing range approached, I half snap rolled, a violent, skidding, turning evolution. He missed. So far so good.

'Craning my neck, I turned in near the stall to keep him in sight and dived again. He climbed gracefully, then peeled off for a repeat peformance. The Zero made five runs. Each time I was lucky enough to produce an opposite course run.

'Finally, ammo expended, he waggled his wings cheerfully, and headed for home. I was in a cold sweat. The reaction hit me; I don't recall the flight back. Theoretical tactics are well and good, but the real McCoy is another matter. From then on, I thought wryly, I was a bomber, period.

'But my good intentions withered at Saipan. The temptation was too great. It happened while on long-range patrol, searching for the Imperial Navy west of Saipan on 18 June. Task Force 58 was screening the amphibious landings in the Marianas.

'Suddenly there was a Jake, fat dumb and

Above: Lt(jg) Charles English Henderson III with his crewmen aboard USS *Enterprise* in 1944. / *Henderson*

as we flashed past. Miraculously, we were untouched by the swirling flames.

'Our team had an unfair advantage. We possessed self-sealing fuel tanks; layers of rubber sealed our tanks when holed. But a few tracers and the Japanese aircraft could explode. Later our chief gunner's mate told me my port gun had jammed; that my starboard gun had fired only 17 rounds.

'So now my appetite was wetted, and once again I became a would-be fighter pilot. And I was lucky. Two days later on long patrol we crossed search patterns with the Imperial fleet. This time I saw a Jill carrier-based torpedo bomber. My TBF was slightly faster than the Jill. After a long tail chase, he finally burned. This was more credit to the manufacturer of my plane than to me as the pilot.'

After Air Group 10 finished its second tour in July 1944, many of the torpedo squadron personnel decided to remain with Cdr Bill Martin and join the new Night Air Group 90. Henderson, still eager and aggressive after two years of war, was among those who signed on for another go, again aboard the 'Big E'.

'My radar operator Ted Halbach and I were convinced that air-to-air interceptions were feasible. A particularly harassing evening with Henry Loomis, the radar expert on Admiral Gardner's staff, convinced me. Henry sneaked away to fly with us at every opportunity.

'Ted and I developed our skill at chasing friendly aircraft. We would contact, then endeavour to close by radar only. Opposite course was the most difficult manoeuvre. The direction, altitude and speed would have to be carefully estimated and our 180° turn timed perfectly to again pick up the target. Our radar was limited by the side angle as well as the vertical angle. Finally, our maximum range — very good for such early airborne radar — was 15 miles. But we were far behind the British and Germans.

'On every mission we searched remorselessly, to the extent of fuel, and never mind the admiral's indignation when we returned late. One night, as we headed home from Kyushu, Ted picked up a bogey. Our moment of truth had arrived.

'It was a dirty, drizzly night in early 1945. The bogey was heading in our direction, slightly above and to starboard. I could see the blip on my repeater scope as Ted coached me in. A cold sweat clammed my back as I followed his terse commands: "Starboard 10 and climb at 150kts. Range three miles."

'The blip was growing larger; a big aircraft dead ahead.

'I charged my guns. My gunsight was a dim hairline on the windscreen.

happy, cruising along far off my port wing, below scattered clouds. I too was fat, dumb and happy. In fact, I had my shoes off, feet up on top of the instrument panel, smoking a cigar. I still don't know what happened to the cigar. All I do know was that I was shortly 90° port, full throttle, guns charged and hands sweating. I knew I'd only have one chance. Cliff Largess was flying my wing, a very eager young man.

'Carefully we eased around above the clouds. He never even saw us as we dived through the cover on his starboard quarter and pulled up in a gentle low side run. The rising sun was prominent on the Jake as I squeezed the button. A short burst. He erupted. A tiny red glow expanded instantly into a ball of fire. I yanked back on my stick

'Carefully, painstakingly we eased up on our victim. One thousand yards and dead ahead, a black void with rain splattering on the canopy. He was cruising at about 140kts and 4,000ft, straight down Kamikaze Alley, the line of islands stretching from Kyushu to Okinawa.

'One hundred yards, a black void. Fifty yards, nothing. My fingers caressed the trigger. I could feel the sweat running down my back, yet it was very cold. Then a blur, darker than the dark, and the tail of a large aircraft appeared like a phantom, the exhaust from his starboard engine sparking the void. I eased forward in tight formation, my port gun behind his starboard engine, manoeuvring into position to fire. The suddenly I saw the blur of his wings — an inverted V!

'So intense was my frustration that I very nearly squeezed the trigger. How dare he not be Japanese! What was a Martin Mariner doing at this time in this place? Clearly he was friendly. Equally clearly, I was not. In truth, I had never in my life felt less friendly.

'Finally I located his frequency on my data sheet. He was from that miserable PBM squadron operating near Okinawa. I called over the radio with a distinct Japanese accent: "All-same looksee starboard side, mellican boy." He pleasured me with a violent diving turn to port as he peeled off for the deck. Thus ended my fifth unfriendly encounter. Ted took it quite well, I raged for days. But at least we now knew we could make an air-to-air intercept with our radar.

'In March 1945, Task Force 58 cruised the coast of Japan, pinning down the airstrips which were launching a steady stream of Kamikazes south to harass our ships. One evening several of us departed *Enterprise* with the pleasant instruction to seek out and destroy convoys in the Inland Sea. Operating singly, as was our custom, I cruised in through Bungo Strait and west towards the Straits of Shimonoseki. Shortly Ted announced a small convoy. We obliged them with eight rockets and four 500lb bombs, the former addressed to their screening destroyer. Pleased with ourselves, and with the safety of it all, we headed home.

'Cruising casually out of Bungo Strait at 4,000ft, we were electrified by Ted's call: "Bandit at 15 miles above, extreme angle, pull up." I did so. And then, "Closing rapidly, slight angle to port. He must be opposite course."

'I turned to compensate and climbed rapidly at full throttle. We manoeuvred for the moment of truth, our 180° turn.

'"Execute!" I could sense his tenseness. And then a breathless silence as I completed my turn, still climbing. Had we failed? Ted was searching frantically. Then a flick on the corner of his scope. He turned me swiftly. There was the bogey, fat and beautiful at 14 miles, still far above us.

'At 12,000ft we levelled off and began to close. It was a long climb. We had to slightly better his cruising speed at all times, and our stripped-down TBM, though very spritely, was no fighter.

'Again it was a dirty night, with light cloud and misty rain, shortly before dawn. Slowly we edged closer, and I charged both my wing guns. At 300yd we couldn't see a thing, like a PBM! I shuddered at the thought of a repeat performance. A giant tail emerged, like a spectre. Then the glow of four engines as I closed in tight formation. An Emily! We had hit the jackpot!

'I locked my port wing behind his starboard outboard engine nacelle and fired. He reacted instantly, turning, weaving, twisting and diving. Grimly I hung on, flying wing on his wing, holding my port gun directly behind his engine nacelle. Time stood still — was endless — was nothing. He strove to shake me off; I clung tenaciously.

'Then I saw the water. We had dropped 12,000ft. After all of our preparations and struggle, we had failed. Better to ram and chop up his tail with my prop. Suddenly I comprehended the Kamikaze spirit.

'And then a sparkle of flame. I squeezed a long burst, perhaps my last. A larger flame, a fire. Swiftly I pulled up and away from a ball of fire, an immense explosion. Awed in spite of ourselves, we viewed the pyre and flames high in the sky.

'I had another theory, namely that rockets would be a good way to shoot down aircraft. We carried eight five-inch rockets. So every day I'd save two, just in case. I'd fire them when I reached our task force outer screen, as it would not do to land with live rockets.

'On this day in May, no sooner did I fire the two rockets I'd been saving then I spotted an enemy fighter. We were near southern Kyushu. It was a Tojo, and he didn't see me so I eased up behind him. If only I had kept those rockets! It was a clear, early morning. At what I judged to be perfect range, I fired. Away he went, smoking but otherwise intact. Another failure.

'I did get a Rufe finally, on 13 May. After a long dogfight I managed to turn inside him thanks to wheels and full flaps down. He plunged into the sea.

'I never did get a chance to prove my rocket theory. A Japanese suicide pilot named Tomi Zai took care to that. On the same day I got my Rufe, he did a beautiful split-S, right out of a cloud above us. He entered the deck abaft number one elevator and blew it hundreds of feet into the air. So the "Big E" went home, this time for good.'

Markings

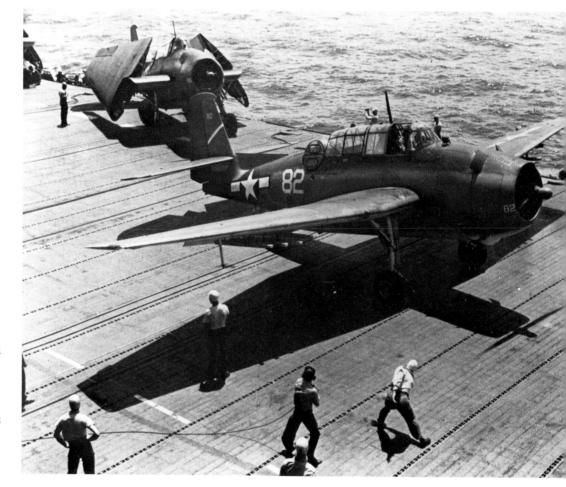

Right: The simple yet
distinctive diagonal tail slash
identified aircraft from the
second *Yorktown* (CV-10)
during 1943-44. This is a
TBF-1C of Torpedo Squadron 1
in June 1944. / *R. M. Hill*

Below: The N prefix and thin
vertical line along the rudder
hinge distinguished these
TBF-1Cs as belonging to VC-63
aboard escort carrier *Natoma
Bay.* They were flying over
Wotje Island on 9 February
1944. / *R. M. Hill*

Top: Mission markers were unusual on carrier aircraft, but this TBF-1C of VT-2 aboard USS *Hornet* was an exception. By early August 1944 the Avenger had completed 53 bombing and three torpedo missions. Reason enough to photograph the plane captain with his charge's record. / *R. M. Hill*

Above: Two thin lines atop the rudder mark this TBM-1 as a VT-26 aircraft off the escort carrier *Santee.* The photo date is 20 October 1944 and in the background is Panson Island. / *R. M. Hill*

Right: Air Group 7 aboard USS *Hancock* employed this distinctive horseshoe insignia during its tour in late 1944. / *R. M. Hill*

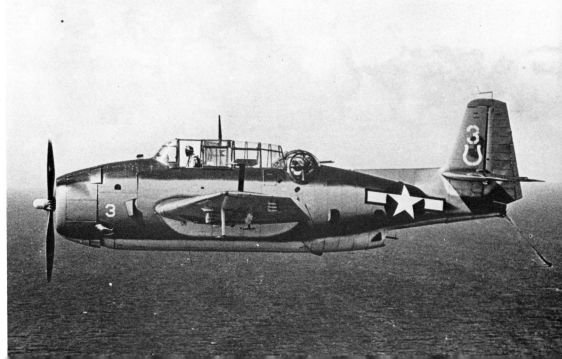

Right: A horizontal white band around the rudder identified USS *Essex* during most of 1944. These TBM-3s of VT-4 are on the first carrier strike against French Indochina, 12 January 1945. / *R. M. Hill*

Below: Torpedo Squadron 20 off USS *Lexington* put its aircraft numbers in black over a white triangle. This VT-20 TBM-3 has just attacked a Japanese convoy in Camranh Bay, French Indochina. / *R. M. Hill*

Bottom: Two Eastern Aircraft products from two escort carriers, A VC-84 TBM-3 off USS *Makin Island* is joined by an FM-2 Wildcat from USS *Lunga Point* in January 1945. / *R. M. Hill*

Right: The 'Christmas tree' marking of USS *Bennington* was carrried by VT-82 during early 1945. / *R. M. Hill*

Below: Air Group 83 succeeded Air Group 4 aboard *Essex*, and brought new markings with it. This TBM-3 of VT-83 launches into a heavy wind on 22 February 1945. / *R. M. Hill*

Bottom: This March 1945 photo shows a fine landing by a VT-45 TBM-3 aboard USS *San Jacinto* on 21 March 1945. Note that the white square of Air Group 45 is repeated on the aircraft's starboard wing-tip.

Left: Composite Squadron 92 used this unusual triangle marking while flying off USS *Tulagi* in early 1945. / *R. M. Hill*

Below left: The escort carrier *Rudyerd Bay* had one of the most distinctive air group symbols of the war. Equally interesting is the mixture of tri-colour and overall gloss blue paint scheme of the TBM-3s of VC-96. All the FM-2s appear to be gloss blue. / *R. M. Hill*

Above right: Dot, a TBM-3 of VT-40 off USS *Suwanee* in April 1945. A few escort carriers had CVE air groups instead of composite squadrons, as evidenced by the F6F Hellcat in the background. All *Suwanee* aircraft at this time carried the letter D prefix. / *R. M. Hill*

Centre right: What better symbol for an anti-submarine aircraft than a fish hook? Composite Squadron 97 used this original marking while flying from escort carrier *Makassar Strait* in 1945. / *R. M. Hill*

Below: Another unusual tail marking was that of VC-8 aboard *Nehenta Bay*. / *R. M. Hill*

Below right: Flight deck repairs proceed uninterrupted aboard *Natoma Bay* as a VC-9 TBM with its white-topped rudder and fin is catapulted on 7 June 1945. / *R. M. Hill*

123

Right: Another variation on the lightning bolt theme. This time the unit is VT-85 from the fleet carrier *Shangri-La.* / *R. M. Hill*

Below: Vertical white lines on the fin and ailerons identify VT-89 off USS *Antietam*, over Shanghai in August 1945. / *R. M. Hill*

Left: A riddle for markings buffs. How did the lead TBM-3 get a gloss blue vertical stabiliser and rudder on a tri-colour scheme airframe? The twin lightning bolts identify the escort carrier *Saginaw Bay*, July 1945. / *National Archives*

Below: In late July the Fast Carrier Force issued one or two-letter tail codes to replace the air group symbols previously used. It was some time before the order was complied with by all ships, but USS *Yorktown* got the job done. Close examination shows the earlier symbols painted over before application of the RR code on these VT-88 TBM-3s. Photo date is 22 August. / *R. M. Hill*

Bottom: Torpedo Squadron 87 aboard USS *Ticonderoga* used this V marking in August 1945, as did the rest of Air Group 87. / *R. M. Hill*

Right: Light carrier *Monterey* was issued the tail code letter C, which was applied to the TBM-3Es of VT-34. Mission insignia and pin-up girl are unusual for carrier aircraft. / R. M. Hill

Below: Escort carriers had their markings standardised in June 1945 with a systematic method of tail and wing patterns. USS *Petrof Bay* used this configuration for the rest of the war. In fact, peace had been declared seven days before this photo was taken on 9 September. / R. M. Hill

Epilogue

Few people — not even those who flew and loved it — would claim the Avenger was the best aircraft of World War II. It was overly heavy, burdened with excess equipment it seldom used. Underpowered, it lacked the speed and performance many aircrew desired.

But despite its shortcomings, the TBF-TBM series was certainly a success. Above all, it was easy to fly, operating safely from every class of carrier in the US Navy. Its roomy interior accepted an increasingly sophisticated assortment of equipment and ordnance, and it had the range to take its payload as far or farther than its escorting fighters could fly. When F6F and F4U squadrons became more numerous aboard fleet carriers in early 1945, the SB2C Helldivers were often removed, but the TBMs remained. The fighters could do a good job of dive-bombing, but there were some things only the Avenger could do properly.

Avengers searched for the enemy until they found him. Then they attacked with bombs, torpedoes, rockets, depth charges: whatever was needed. From 1942 to 1945 TBFs and TBMs helped sink about 60 Japanese warships. And between these sorties they delivered mail, ferried personnel, hauled contraband liquor and frequently offered a shady place to sleep.

Of comparable importance is the fact that the TBF and TBM were produced in larger numbers than any other carrier-based strike aircraft — nearly 10,000 in all. They were found from Midway to Guadalcanal, from Saigon to Tokyo, from Morocco to Norway.

And the Avenger enjoyed a long service life. When the last TBM-3Es were withdrawn from VS-27 in October of 1954, the series had been in use for $12\frac{1}{2}$ years. At the time it was a record for longevity unmatched in the US Navy.

But with all the varieties of missions and locales, the Avenger's greatest contribution was undoubtedly in the Atlantic. Its role in defeating the U-boat wolfpacks was an important factor in winning the war in Europe. While other aircraft played prominent parts in the anti-submarine campaign, none of them performed so wide variety of roles as well as the Avenger: detecting, stalking, killing and discouraging U-boats by day and night. Because of the escort carriers and their aircraft, sea communications were kept open between the Old World and the New. Otherwise, the Normandy invasion would never have been possible.

Despite its wide success, no individual TBF or TBM is well known to history. Unlike Cdr David McCampbell's Hellcat *Minsi III* or the B-17 *Memphis Belle*, there existed no real-life Avenger to catch the public's fancy. Instead, the best-known TBF remains an imaginary one — the battered, ageing relic known as *The Bouncing Belch* in James Michener's marvellous novel, *Tales of the South Pacific*. The Belch was flown by Lt Bus Adams, a cynical, skilful aviator lovingly cast as part hero, part heel. Both the plane and the pilot were ficticious, but like the steel and aluminium Avengers and the flesh and blood men who flew them, they remain unforgettable.

Right: **TBMs and SB2Cs of Air Group 84 off USS *Bunker Hill* on a strike in 1945.**
/ National Archives

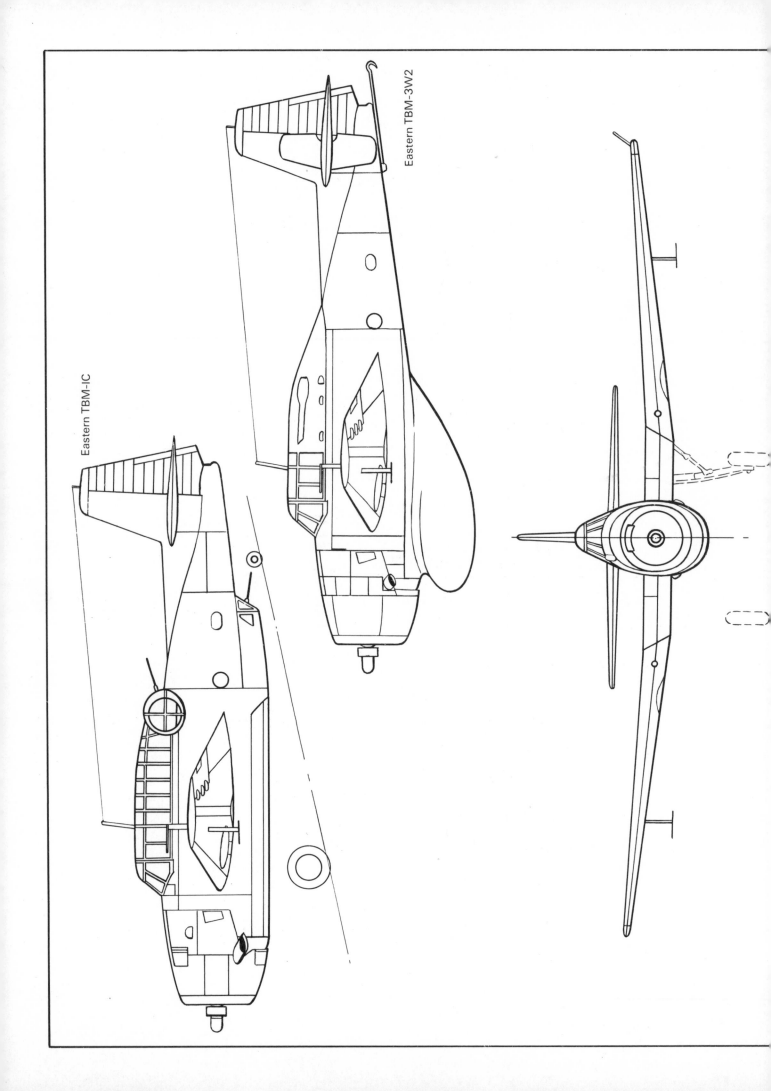

Eastern TBM-3W2

Eastern TBM-IC